The Price Waterhouse
Personal Tax Strategy

1996 EDITION

Canadian Cataloguing in Publication Data

The National Library of Canada has catalogued this publication as follows:

Personal tax strategy (Canadian ed.)
   Personal tax strategy

Annual.
ISSN 1189-0169
ISBN 0-385-25575-6 (1996)

1. Income tax — Canada — Popular works.
I. Price Waterhouse (Firm).   II. Title: The Price
Waterhouse personal tax strategy

HJ4661.P463   343.7105'1'05   C91-032798-X

Cover design by Avril Orloff
Cover illustration by Mike Custode
Text design by David Montle
Information graphics concept and design by Price Waterhouse
Printed and bound in the USA

Published in Canada by
Doubleday Canada Limited
105 Bond Street
Toronto, Ontario
M5B 1Y3

Personal Tax Strategy is intended to provide information that is accurate,
comprehensible and useful. This book, however, is not a substitute for legal
or accounting advice, which should be obtained from competent professionals
before important tax planning decisions are made. Please see the section
"Beyond this book" on page 7 for further information.

The Price Waterhouse Personal Tax Strategy

1996 EDITION

Doubleday Canada Limited

Personal Tax Calendar

This Personal Tax Calendar shows key **tax deadlines**, indicating the day of the month for 1996. (Some dates change slightly from year to year.) The calendar also raises **planning reminders** that may need consideration.

To avoid missing deadlines or valuable planning opportunities, **check this calendar periodically**. You may want to add your own tax-related dates and planning reminders.

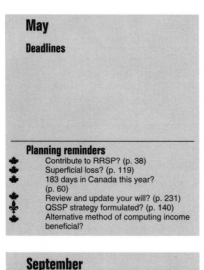

January

Deadlines

★ 15 Fourth U.S. estimated tax payment for prior year
🍁 30 Interest on employee and family loans (p. 23)
🍁 31 Inform employer of personal use of car
★ 31 File U.S. tax return if owed estimated tax on January 15 but did not pay (to avoid penalty)

Planning reminders

🍁 Contribute to RRSP – for last year and this year? (p. 38)
🍁 Superficial loss? (p. 119)
🍁 Use Home Buyers' Plan (p. 227)

February

Deadlines

🍁 14 Reimburse employer for personal automobile expenses
● 15 Last day to file for withholding tax exemption
🍁 29 RRSP contribution in respect of prior year (p. 38)

Planning reminders

🍁 Expecting a tax refund? File early. (p. 193)
🍁 Slips and receipts to assemble?
🍁 Alternative method of computing income beneficial?
🍁 Review and update your will? (p. 231)
🍁 Use Home Buyers' Plan (p. 227)

May

Deadlines

Planning reminders

🍁 Contribute to RRSP? (p. 38)
🍁 Superficial loss? (p. 119)
🍁 183 days in Canada this year? (p. 60)
🍁 Review and update your will? (p. 231)
⚜ QSSP strategy formulated? (p. 140)
🍁 Alternative method of computing income beneficial?

June

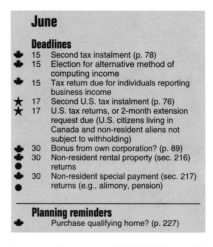

Deadlines

🍁 15 Second tax instalment (p. 78)
🍁 15 Election for alternative method of computing income
🍁 15 Tax return due for individuals reporting business income
★ 17 Second U.S. tax instalment (p. 76)
★ 17 U.S. tax returns, or 2-month extension request due (U.S. citizens living in Canada and non-resident aliens not subject to withholding)
🍁 30 Bonus from own corporation? (p. 89)
🍁● 30 Non-resident rental property (sec. 216) returns
🍁● 30 Non-resident special payment (sec. 217) returns (e.g., alimony, pension)

Planning reminders

🍁 Purchase qualifying home? (p. 227)

September

Deadlines

🍁 15 Third tax instalment (p. 76)
★ 16 Third U.S. estimated tax payment
🍁 30 Acquire home if Home Buyers' Plan withdrawal made in 1995 (p. 227)

Planning reminders

🍁 Superficial loss? (p. 119)
🍁 Contributing to charities or political parties? (p.188)
🍁 CNIL problems to eliminate? (p.115)

October

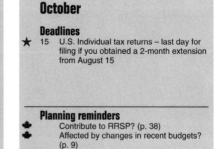

Deadlines

★ 15 U.S. Individual tax returns – last day for filing if you obtained a 2-month extension from August 15

Planning reminders

🍁 Contribute to RRSP? (p. 38)
🍁 Affected by changes in recent budgets? (p. 9)
🍁 Moving soon? (p. 32)
🍁 183 days in Canada this year? (p. 60)
🍁 CNIL problems to eliminate? (p.115)

The symbols beside each deadline or planning question indicate the relevant jurisdiction.

🍁 Canada   ⚜ Québec only   ★ U.S.   ● International

March

Deadlines
🍁 15   First tax instalment (p. 76)
🍁 30   Trust returns and preferred beneficiary elections (p. 235)

Planning reminders
🍁   Expecting a tax refund? File early. (p. 193)
🍁   Slips and receipts to assemble?
🍁   Superficial loss? (p. 119)
🍁   Affected by changes in recent budgets? (p. 9)

April

Deadlines
★ 15   US tax return or 4-month extension request due, or file for extension for non-resident aliens (subject to withholding)
★ 15   First US estimated tax payment
★ 15   US Trust and Partnership Returns or 3-month extension request due
🍁 30   File tax return (p. 210)

Planning reminders
🍁   Alternative method of computing income beneficial?
🍁   Purchase qualifying home? (p. 227)

July

Deadlines
★ 15   U.S. Trust and Partnership returns – filing deadline if automatic 3-month extension obtained.

Planning reminders
🍁   Superficial loss? (p. 119)
🍁   Claiming enhanced capital gains exemption? (p. 91)
🍁   Moving soon? (p. 32)
🍁   Objecting to a notice of (re)assessment? (p. 213)

August

Deadlines
★ 15   U.S. Individual tax returns – last day for filing if you obtained a 4-month extension

Planning reminders
🍁   Review and update your will? (p. 231)
🍁   Contribute to RRSP? (p. 38)
🍁   Purchase qualifying home? (p. 227)

November

Deadlines
🍁 1   Canada Savings Bonds

Planning reminders
🍁   Superficial loss? (p. 119)
🍁   Claiming enhanced capital gains exemption? (p. 225)
🍁   CNIL problems to eliminate? (p. 115)
⚜   Any QSSP transactions required? (p. 140)

December

Deadlines
🍁 15   Fourth tax instalment (p. 76)
🍁 31   Expenses to claim (p. 84)
🍁 31   RPP contributions (p. 34)
🍁 31   RRSP conversion at age 71 (p. 147)
🍁 31   Car operating benefit election (p. 50)
★ 31   Fourth state estimated tax payment for deduction in year just ending

Planning reminders
🍁   Contributing to charities or political parties? (p. 188)
⚜   CNIL problems to eliminate? (p. 115)
⚜   QSSP strategy complete? (p. 140)

Contents

A detailed table of contents appears
at the beginning of each chapter.

Calculating Your Taxes

Filing Returns and Paying Your Taxes

Looking Ahead

Appendices

Glossary of Abbreviations   266

Index   269

Introduction

Using this book – special features

This book has several features to make personal tax planning easier. It has a chapter especially for you if you are:

- an employee;
- an investor;
- an owner/manager;
- retired;
- separated or divorced
- a taxpayer with U.S. connections.

Issues that could affect all taxpayers are covered in sections on:

- 1995 highlights;
- significant cases;
- calculating your taxes;
- filing returns and paying your taxes;
- looking ahead.

This year's **tax highlights** and recent significant court **cases** are set out on pages 9 to 19.

Each chapter has a **distinctive graphic icon**, which appears at the top of each right-hand page of the chapter. The chapters begin with "What's new" — one or more highlights of recent tax-related changes.

Throughout the book, **international aspects** are marked by a stylized globe (like the one in the margin here). Numerous tax tips highlight valuable tax-saving techniques.

A **detailed table of contents at the beginning of each chapter** helps you find topics that interest you. An **Index** is also provided.

Québec taxpayers have to deal with not only the federal system but a different provincial tax regime. At the end of each chapter, a special **Québec section** sets out tax matters that are significantly different in that province. Each Québec section is marked by a fleur-de-lis in the margin and at the top of the right-hand page.

Key tax numbers are collected in **appendices**. Graphs and tables present information in an easily digestible form in the appendices and throughout the text. The **Personal Tax Flowchart** on pages 183 and 193 gives you the "big picture", revealing the components and structure of your income tax calculation.

Tax matters involve numerous abbreviations such as AMT and CNIL. A **glossary** (page 266) decodes them.

You'll find the **Personal Tax Calendar** before the table of contents of this book. Referring to your Personal Tax Calendar several times throughout the year will remind you of tax planning opportunities as well as important deadlines.

Developing Your
Personal Tax Strategy

Developing Your Personal Tax Strategy

Your personal tax strategy is important. This introductory chapter outlines steps you should consider to begin your tax planning, and explains the features of this book that can help you.

Why develop a personal tax strategy?

Investing time in your personal tax strategy can help you minimize your taxes, both short-term and long-term. You may be able to cut your tax bill by:

- reducing the amount payable this year; and

- deferring payment until a later year.

Cash flow management is part of a good personal tax strategy. The success of your tax plan, whether it is basic or complex, may be undetermined if you do not give enough consideration to cash flow issues.

Make sure that you refer to the chapter **Filing Returns and Paying Your Taxes** (page 203). You may find that you can save some money, or at least improve cash flow, by applying some of the simple tactics described in that chapter, both at tax time and throughout the year. For example, managing your instalment payments or reducing the tax withheld from your paycheque may leave you with more discretionary income with which to implement some of your tax strategies — or just to save or spend.

It is probably a good idea to review the **Significant Cases: an overview** section that follows **1995 Highlights** (page 12). You may be able to take a favourable filing position on an issue decided on by the courts that is similar to one you are dealing with yourself. Alternatively, you may find that you have to adjust a prior year's return if a decision on which you based a particular filing position has subsequently been reversed. Before taking any action on jurisprudence that you believe may be relevant in your own situation, consider discussing your conclusions with your professional advisor.

This book will show you the many advantages of tax planning. Now may be a good time to get started.

Getting the most out of this book

You can use this book to:

- reduce your tax bill by identifying tax planning opportunities to implement yourself or with professional advice;

- understand the process of preparing your income tax return, whether you do it or have it done for you; and

- save time and money by answering many of your questions and focusing your attention.

Beginning your tax planning

To begin your tax planning:

- Review your 1994 returns and assessments to help you recall the sources of your income and the deductions you have claimed.

- Note extraordinary transactions, events or amounts for later consideration and possible special action.

- Review the section **Significant cases: an overview** on page 12. You may find that a recent court decision has an effect on your own tax situation.

- Estimate your 1995 taxable income by calculating your income and deductions, using your 1994 return and this book as guides (see "Calculating your taxes" page 179).

6

- Check your liability for tax instalments. If your tax deductions at source do not cover most of your total tax liability, you may be required to make quarterly instalments. If you are required to make instalments of tax, Revenue Canada or Revenue Québec should already have sent you notices for each of your four 1995 instalments. You may pay your instalments according to this system, or, you may use the method you have used in the past. As long as you base your instalments on the Revenue Canada or Revenue Québec notices and pay your instalments on time, you won't be charged interest and penalties, even if your payments fall short of your total tax liability for the year. If you missed any instalment payments that were required during the year, you can minimize charges by making a catch-up payment now. (See page 209.)

- On the Personal Tax Calendar (page iv), mark any dates and planning points that apply to you. On your own calendar, mark a few reminders to review the Personal Tax Calendar. Use this book to identify planning techniques and to help you assess tax saving opportunities.

- Balance the cash flow requirements of possible deferral techniques against the potential for reduced tax.

- If you disagree with the re-assessment for 1994 or a prior year, dispute it by discussing it with Revenue Canada or Revenue Québec and perhaps by filing a Notice of Objection (see page 220). A disagreement can invalidate the amounts for your quarterly instalments specified in Revenue Canada or Revenue Québec notices.

After completing your analysis, consider discussing your conclusions with a professional advisor.

Start now

To get the most out of *Personal Tax Strategy*, don't wait until your tax return is almost due before looking through it for tax planning opportunities — start now. Use whatever approach works best for you: for example, flip through the pages, scan the table of contents or start with the Personal Tax Calendar on page iv. Then zero-in on material that applies to you.

Use *Personal Tax Strategy* throughout the year

Personal Tax Strategy is a planning tool, so you may want to refer to it several times throughout the year. That's why we suggest marking a few dates in your own calendar. On those dates, a glance at the Personal Tax Calendar will remind you of important tax-related deadlines and planning opportunities.

Use *Personal Tax Strategy* at tax time

When the time comes to prepare your tax return, *Personal Tax Strategy* will help you understand how the various entries are related and why they are calculated the way they are. *Personal Tax Strategy* complements the tax guides that the taxation authorities provide, which help you with the details of filling out your return.

Beyond this book

This book is no substitute for competent professional advice. Tax planning is a complex process that must be tailored to your circumstances. Accordingly, the comments and advice in this book are not intended to be a definitive analysis of the law, but rather to guide you in understanding some of the ways to minimize your tax burden.

Throughout *Personal Tax Strategy* you will encounter references

8 to the 1995 federal and provincial budget proposals, as well as to other draft legislation and technical amendments. How should you deal with rules that are still just proposals or drafts? Usually, you should assume that these measures will become law, whether they give or take away your opportunity to do something.

If you are considering implementing a complex tax plan, or when significant amounts are involved, you should consult your professional advisor before proceeding.

Effective dates for implementation are provided for particular changes or proposals.

This book is based on:

- legislation enacted up to the end of October 31, 1995;

- technical amendments to the Income Tax Act released in April and July 1995;

- Department of Finance Press Releases announced up to October 31, 1995;

- proposals in provincial budgets or information releases up to August 31, 1995 (all provinces had presented their 1995-96 budgets when *Personal Tax Strategy* was written); and

- the Protocol to amend the Canada-U.S. Tax Convention, expected to be ratified in November 1995.

Post-publication changes in the interpretation of the law or in the Department of National Revenue's administrative policy could affect the information in this book.

Additional information on any of the matters discussed in *Personal Tax Strategy* is available from any Price Waterhouse office in Canada. See pages 267-68 for addresses.

1996 Highlights

To assess your overall personal tax position, you should review the changes that come into effect each year and understand how they could alter your tax planning. The tax changes highlighted below, along with their general implications, will help you see how you may be affected.

A number of personal tax changes introduced in the 1995 federal budget will affect your personal tax planning. You will likely want to review carefully the proposed changes to tax assisted retirement savings, particularly if you have overcontributed to your RRSP or will be receiving a retiring allowance. If you are self-employed, you will want to consider the effect of the proposed rules requiring you to report your business or professional income on a calendar year basis. Finally, proposed increases to interest charged on overdue taxes, including instalments, will make late and deficient payments more expensive than ever.

The 1994 federal budget measure eliminating the $100,000 lifetime capital gains exemption may still affect you. Although you will be subject to a penalty, opportunities remain to shelter capital gains that accrued up to February 22, 1994 with any unused capital gains exemption.

The provinces left personal income tax rates virtually untouched in their 1995 budgets. Residents of Ontario will be looking with interest to their new government and the status of campaign promises to lower personal tax rates. The appendices at the end of this book (page 239) provide more detail on income tax rates.

Tax changes	Implications for you
	Higher tax bills
There is a small "hidden" federal tax increase for 1995: the tax brackets and your personal and other credits will be the same in 1995 as they were in 1994 (indeed, the tax brackets and most credits have remained unchanged since 1992).	The tax brackets and credits increase from one year to the next to the extent that the increase in the Consumer Price Index exceeds 3%. Although the good news is that inflation was less than 3%, if your income increased by at least the rate of inflation, you will face a higher tax bite.
The $100,000 lifetime capital gains exemption was eliminated for capital gains realized after February 22, 1994.	The deadline for filing an election to shelter a portion of capital gains that accrued up to February 22, 1994 was April 30, 1995. There is still an opportunity to take advantage of the election. Penalties will generally apply, however, to late filed elections.
The 1995 federal budget proposes to increase the rate of interest charged on late or deficient income tax payments.	Paying your taxes late is going to be costlier than ever: the current rate of interest charged on overdue taxes, insufficient instalments, unpaid employee source deductions, etc. will be increased by an additional two percent. The rate paid by the government on refunds remains unchanged.

	Lower tax bills
The 1995 federal budget proposes to exempt qualified donations of ecologically sensitive land from the annual limit of 20 percent of net income.	The value of donated land may often be high relative to a donor's income. Accordingly, the 20 percent rule may restrict the value of the donation credit, even after the five-year carryforward. The exemption from the 20 percent of net income limit is intended to encourage the conservation and protection of Canada's environmental heritage.

	Retirement savings
Changes to pensions and RRSPs were announced in the 1995 federal budget.	You won't be able to contribute the maximum $15,500 to your RRSP until 1999. The $8,000 overcontribution allowance will be reduced to $2,000 in 1996. The rollover of retiring allowances to RRSPs will be phased out after 1995.

	Tax change	Implications for you
Retirement savings	Changes to the taxation of Old Age Security benefits will come into effect July 1996.	OAS benefits will be paid on the basis of your previous year's income. Rather than being clawed back on your tax return, OAS payments will be reduced before they are sent out to you. Non-residents of Canada will have to file a statement of worldwide income in order to receive OAS benefits.
Business and professional income	Deferral advantages for business and professional income have been eliminated by proposals in the 1995 federal budget.	For taxation years starting after 1994, you will be required to report business and professional income on a calendar year basis, i.e., you will no longer be able to choose a non-calendar year end for tax purposes.
Tax shelters	Draft legislation released on April 26, 1995 proposes measures to limit the use of tax shelters.	The proposed rules are targeted at limited recourse financings. The effect of the proposal is to limit losses that are deductible in respect of a tax shelter.
Other topics	Changes were announced in the 1995 federal budget that will affect the taxation of family trusts.	The election to defer the application of the 21-year rule will be eliminated January 1, 1999. Further, the preferred beneficiary election has been repealed for taxation years of trusts commencing after 1995.
	The Protocol amending the Canada-U.S. tax treaty was signed on March 17, 1995. It is expected to be ratified in November 1995.	The Protocol means some reduced withholding rates, relief from tax treatment of cross-border pension and social security payments, and fairer U.S. estate tax liabilities for Canadians.
	If you own a rental or commercial building in Québec, you will have to disclose payments made to specified persons. A lessor of a commercial building must also make these disclosures.	You will need to collect the requisite information from the company or individual working for you on your building.

12 | Significant cases: an overview

An in-depth discussion of the jurisprudence dealing with income tax issues over the last year or so is beyond the scope of Personal Tax Strategy. However, some court decisions relate specifically to the material in this book. A brief overview of several important decisions follows. Many cases dealt with topics such as the deductibility of business losses and the disability credit; these are discussed in more general terms.

If you intend to take a filing position based on any of these decisions, discuss your plans with your professional advisor first. Your situation may not be parallel to the case you have in mind, or the decision you consider favourable may have been reversed on appeal.

Employee relocation reimbursements

Refer to page 29 for a discussion of employee relocation reimbursements.

Tuition fees – employment benefit

A bank employee attended a university executive MBA program. He initiated the request to be allowed to participate in the program, but it was within his employer's human resource policy to encourage certain employees to attend such programs. His employer reimbursed him for the tuition paid by him (in excess of $28,000) and included it in his T4 slip. When the individual filed his tax return, he excluded the amount reimbursed by the bank for the tuition. The court agreed with Revenue Canada: the amount was clearly a taxable benefit from employment and must be included in income for tax purposes.

Relevant case: *Sami, Jim H. v. The Queen* (June 26, 1995, file #94-2938[IT]I — unreported)

Possible implications for you: Amounts that you receive from your employer, unless specifically excluded by provisions in the Income Tax Act, must be included in your income for tax purposes as income from employment. Generally, this is true even if you believe the payments do not have anything directly to do with your employment duties. If you received or enjoyed a benefit because of your employee-employer relationship, it is probably employment income.

If you are going to receive payments or reimbursements from your employer that are outside normal remuneration parameters, consider discussing the situation with your professional advisor. There may be alternative ways of structuring a payment. This is particularly important if amounts are significant.

Employment benefit – housing arrangement

The taxpayer received a payment from his employer under a buy-out agreement related to an employee housing arrangement. Under the program, the company agreed to buy back the employee's house, or to pay the employee the real estate commission that would be due if the employee decided to sell the house on the open market. The taxpayer opted into the buy-back program. Six years into the program, the employer decided it no longer wanted to be in the housing market and it established an Early Termination of Agreement Program ("ETAP"). Under the ETAP program, employees who participated in the buy-back program were paid an amount equal to the real estate commission that would be due if the house were sold at current market prices. The taxpayer argued that the amount was not an employment benefit because it arose from a surrender of rights in contract. The Federal Court of Appeal held that the payment was a benefit from employment because it was clearly intended to assist the employees and could not be totally divorced from the employment relationship. The court also found that the

14

buy-back arrangement was an inducement to the taxpayer to accept the employment.

Relevant case: *The Queen v. Blanchard, Eugene Joseph,* 95 DTC 5479 (FCA)

Possible implications for you: See the implications under **Tuition fees — employment benefit** above.

Moving expenses

To deduct moving expenses, an individual must move to a new residence that is at least 40 kilometres closer than a former residence to his or her new work location. The issue in this case was how distance is to be measured if the Income Tax Act does not specify a particular method. The taxpayer measured the distance between her new home and her work by using the odometer on her car. The Tax Court of Canada agreed with Revenue Canada and held that a straight line measurement, i.e., "as the crow flies" is to be used. This case is interesting in that it is the first time that a higher court — the Federal Court of Appeal ("FCA") — has been called upon to consider this issue. The FCA found that the straight line method bears no relation to how an employee actually travels to work. Instead, the Court found that a realistic measurement of travelling distance is necessary and held that the appropriate test is the shortest normal route, i.e., a test that combines the shortest route one might travel to work and a recognition of the normal route available to the travelling public.

Relevant case: *Giannakopoulos, Dianne M. v. MNR,* 95 DTC 5477 (FCA)

Possible implications for you: If you will be moving your residence in order to be closer to a new work location, consider the effect of this decision. You may discover that you are entitled to claim moving expenses because the trip to your new work premises is 40 kilometres closer than from your former home using the actual distance travelled test rather than the "as the crow flies" test.

Business losses

Numerous cases dealing with the deductibility of business losses, including farm losses, were heard over the last year. With few exceptions, the courts found in favour of the Crown. The main reasons for the findings were threefold: no reasonable expectation of profit, unreasonable expenses and inadequate supporting documentation.

If claims for farm losses were involved, the courts found that in general, even though taxpayers had contributed significant time, effort and capital to farming operations, there was either no reasonable expectation of profit or the farming business was subordinate to a taxpayer's means of livelihood.

In the few cases in which the taxpayer was successful, the courts found that even though there were start-up costs and losses, there was reasonable expectation of profit. The courts also found in favour of the taxpayer if the loss experience was too brief to establish the fact of profitability.

Relevant cases: *Hugill, R. v. The Queen*, 95 DTC 5311 (FCA); *Huber, A. v. The Queen*, 95 DTC 5248 (FCA); *Zalzalah, Luay v. The Queen*, 95 DTC 5498 (FCTD); *Stecko, G., v. The Queen*, 95 DTC 5215 (FCTD); *Fearn, R.W. v. The Queen*, 95 DTC 5052 (FCTD); *Rothgeb, R.R. v. The Queen*, 94 DTC 6703 (FCTD); *Waskowec, P. v. The Queen*, 94 DTC 6708 (FCTD)

Possible implications for you: To successfully substantiate a deduction for business losses, ensure that:

16

- you have a bona fide business, (i.e., not something that is entered into for personal reasons or solely for tax purposes);

- you have a reasonable expectation of profit based on sound planning, realistic estimates of receipts and expenditures and monitoring of, and adjustment to, market conditions; and

- your documentation is adequate, complete and in order.

Principal residence

The taxpayer owned a parcel of land that was 32.755 acres, approximately 3 acres of which were around the house and were used for her personal use. The remainder was rented to a farmer. The taxpayer sold the entire parcel for $1.8 million and claimed the whole parcel as part of her principal residence, with the result that the entire gain on sale was not taxable. The local municipal bylaw required a minimum lot area of 25 acres for farming and required a minimum lot area of 20,000 square feet for a building lot with a one family house. Residential uses could be obtained only by consent under the Ontario Planning Act. In a majority decision, the court found that had the taxpayer decided she wanted to divide the property into lots of the size permitted by the regulations, she would have needed the consent of the local authorities and, according to expert testimony, the local authority would not have authorized a partition. The court found that the entire parcel of land was necessary to the taxpayer's use and enjoyment, so she was entitled to favourable tax treatment, i.e., the entire parcel of land was considered to be part of her principal residence.

Relevant case: *Carlile, Grace M. v. The Queen,* 95 DTC 5483 (FCA)

Possible implications for you: Although the principal residence exemption is quite straightforward for a dwelling on a "normal" size lot, the calculation of the exemption for residences that are located on large parcels of land may be subject to restrictions. In instances involving property of greater than ½ hectare (the normal size lot for principal residence exemption purposes), the tax treatment will depend on the particular circumstances and will be determined on a case by case basis. Indeed, the final result may depend on whether it can be established that the excess land is necessary for the use and enjoyment of the residence and on criteria such as ability to subdivide property, local zoning laws, etc.

Interest versus capital gain

The taxpayer purchased a Treasury Bill (T-Bill) at a discount and held it to its maturity. In his tax return, the taxpayer made a Canadian securities election, which generally allows you to treat transactions in Canadian securities to be on account of capital. Accordingly, he treated the difference between the purchase price for the T-Bill and the amount received on maturity as a capital gain. Revenue Canada assessed the proceeds on maturity of the T-Bill as a blended payment of interest and principal. The Courts agreed that the discount on the T-Bill was interest.

Relevant case: *Satinder, K.P. v. The Queen,* 95 DTC 5340 (FCA)

Possible implications for you: The discount on T-Bills is interest income for tax purposes and any amount received on maturity in excess of cost fully taxable. As confirmed by the courts, a Canadian securities election does not change that rule. A T-Bill that is sold prior to maturity, however, may have an element of gain or loss if interest rates changed between the time of acquisition and disposition.

| 18 | ## Alimony and maintenance |

The Supreme Court of Canada heard the Suzanne Thibaudeau case dealing with child support payments. Refer to page 159 for further details about this controversial decision.

A selection of other decisions reinforce the requirement that alimony and maintenance payments, to be deductible, must be periodic, it must be an allowance (i.e., its disposition must be at the entire discretion of the recipient) and it must be pursuant to a written court order or judgment. A hand written agreement between the parties is not sufficient. Further, an agreement must be registered.

For payments to third parties (for example, mortgage and property taxes on the family home) to be deductible to the payer, the amounts must be specified in the agreement and it must be stipulated that they are deductible to the payer and includable in the income of the person on whose behalf the payments are made.

Relevant cases: *The Queen v. Thibaudeau,* 95 DTC 5273 (SCC); *Ambler, Brian v. The Queen,* 95 DTC 5401 (FCA); *Chabros, J. v. The Queen,* 95 DTC 5247 (FCA)

Possible implications for you:

It cannot be stressed too many times: if you are in the midst of negotiations as a result of a marriage breakdown, professional advice from your tax advisor is at least as important as from your lawyer.

Legal fees – support payments

A taxpayer deducted legal expenses that she incurred to successfully contest a motion by her former husband to rescind a support order. The taxpayer's claim was allowed: the legal expenses were deductible since they were incurred in order to obtain payment of income to which she was entitled.

Relevant case: *The Attorney General v. Sembinelli, N. McCready,* 94 DTC 6636 (FCA)

Disability credit

A plethora of cases dealt with the disability credit, either for the taxpayer or for a claim in respect of a taxpayer's spouse or child. For the most part, the courts interpreted quite strictly the requirement that in order to qualify for the credit, an individual's basic activities of daily living must be markedly restricted. It was acknowledged in numerous cases that a taxpayer suffered a severe and prolonged impairment of some nature. The critical issue, however, was whether the individual's basic activities of daily living were markedly restricted. Again, a distinction was made between moderately and markedly restricted, with no credit allowed in the former case. For the most part, assistance to walk, feed, dress and eliminate was necessary to be entitled to the credit.

Relevant cases: *Taylor, J.D. v. The Queen,* 95 DTC 5051 (FCA); *Brown, N.E. v. The Queen,* 95 DTC 5126 (FCTD)

Possible implications for you: A severe and prolonged impairment, while acknowledged by the courts, is not sufficient to entitle you to the disability credit for yourself, your spouse or a dependent child. The onus is on the taxpayer to demonstrate that the basic activities of daily living are markedly restricted.

Employees

Employees

What's new?

- RRSP and RPP contribution limits are to be reduced (proposed).
- RRSP overcontribution allowance is to be reduced to $2,000 (proposed).
- Retiring allowance rollovers are to be phased out (proposed).

For most employees, salary is the main component of income. Employment benefits are often a major component too. The T4 slip that your employer mails to you provides the tax information you need, and the tax consequences of salary are straightforward. Salary is generally taxed when received. However, if your salary is deferred and one of the main reasons is to postpone payment of tax, special rules impose tax on the amount deferred.

In addition to being an employee, you may also be a director, either of another corporation or of the corporation for which you work. If you are a director and are earning directors' fees, those fees are also considered to be employment income and must be included on your tax return. Directors' fees are "earned income" for the purposes of determining how much you can contribute to your own or a spousal RRSP. Refer to page 218 as well for a discussion concerning directors' liability.

Taxable benefits and employment deductions claim most of the attention. Company cars are a major topic on their own, and are dealt with on page 47. Other taxable benefits, nontaxable benefits, and employment deductions (including pension, RRSP and DPSP contributions) are covered first.

Taxable benefits

You must include the value of any taxable benefits received during the year as a result of employment in your income from employment. The most important taxable benefits are company cars, employee loans, and stock options. Frequent flyer points also deserve some attention.

Employee loans

Generally, if your employer makes a loan to you or to a member of your family and charges little or no interest, you receive a taxable benefit. The benefit is computed as the interest on the loan at a pre-scribed rate, less any interest you actually paid within the year or 30 days after year end. The table shows the 1995 prescribed rates for these loans. Rates are subject to adjustment every quarter to reflect market interest rates.

		Prescribed rate for deemed interest on employee and shareholder loans*	* For prescribed rates for overdue taxes, penalties, refunds, etc. see the table on page 77.
Quarter of 1995	1st	6%	
	2nd	8%	
	3rd	9%	
	4th	7%	

If you use the loan proceeds for investment purposes, the loan may be essentially tax-free, since the benefit is offset by an interest expense deduction equal to the amount of the benefit.

The taxable benefit on a loan to acquire a home that you will occupy, or to refinance a mortgage on your current home, is calcu-lated using the lesser of the prescribed interest rate in effect at the time the loan was made or renewed, and the current prescribed rate. These loans are considered to be renewed every five years.

The five-year renewal rule allows you to have the best of both worlds if you benefit from a loan from your employer to purchase a home. For example, assume you received a low interest or interest-free loan from your employer last year when the prescribed rate was five percent. It is now a year later and the rate has increased to nine percent. Your employment benefit is calculated using the five percent rate even though the prescribed rate has increased significantly. If the prescribed rate had dropped, however, the benefit would have been calculated using the lower rate. If you can negotiate a housing loan from your employer as part of your compensation package, this rule can result in a very attractive benefit.

Tax Tip 1

If you started work at a new job in Canada that involved moving within Canada to a home at least 40 kilometres closer to your new work location, the interest benefit on the first $25,000 of a home relocation loan will be tax-free. This exemption is available for the first five years of the loan. You must still report the full amount of the interest benefit. The special deduction for interest on a home relocation loan must be claimed as a separate item on your tax return.

Tax Tip 2

If you change employers within five years of receiving a home relocation loan and your new employer provides you with a loan to repay your former employer, the replacement loan is considered to be the same as the original loan. As long as the replacement loan does not exceed the amount of the original loan, you will be entitled to the special deduction as though the original loan were still in place.

Stock options

Stock options that you get from your employer are taxed differently depending on whether or not the corporation is a Canadian-controlled private corporation (CCPC). In either case, you face no immediate income tax consequences when you receive an employee stock option.

If your employer is not a CCPC, when you exercise an option you are deemed to have received income from employment equal to the difference between the fair market value of the stock when the option is exercised and the total amount you paid to acquire the option and the shares themselves. You may deduct one-quarter of this deemed benefit from your taxable income, so long as the options are qualifying stock options granted after February 15, 1984. Consequently, just three-quarters of the benefit received on the exercise of these options will be taxable as employment income.

A stock option is a "qualifying option" if the exercise price for the related shares is not less than their fair market value when the option is granted, the employee deals at arm's length with the corporation, and the shares under the option arrangement are common shares meeting specific criteria.

The first criterion is applied without reference to fluctuations in the value of a foreign currency relative to the Canadian dollar during the period between the acquisition of the option and the time the share is acquired. Accordingly, when the stock options are denominated in a foreign currency, the deduction will not be denied by reason only of a foreign exchange fluctuation.

On a subsequent sale of the shares, three-quarters of any gain accruing after the exercise date is treated as a taxable capital gain.

Stock options granted to employees of CCPCs are not subject to tax until they dispose of shares. When you dispose of shares in a CCPC, the difference between the fair market value of the shares at the time the option was exercised and the total amount you paid to acquire the options and the shares themselves is treated as employment income. One-quarter of this amount is deductible in arriving at taxable income, provided you have held the shares for at least two years. As with options in non-CCPCs, three-quarters of any gain on the sale of the shares accruing after the exercise date is treated as a taxable capital gain.

Taxable capital gains realized on the disposition of shares that you acquired when you exercised stock options will generally be subject to tax. The $100,000 lifetime capital gains exemption was eliminated for gains realized or accrued after February 22, 1994. An election filed with your 1994 tax return was generally your last chance to use up any general capital gains exemption that you had available to you. If you did not make the election and you owned shares with accrued gains on February 22, 1994, you may still have an opportunity to shelter a portion of the gains. Late elections may be filed within two years of the April 30, 1995 filing deadline, provided a penalty is paid (see page 107 for further details about the capital gains exemption election and late filing penalties).

Special rules are provided to take care of problems that could arise if CCPC options were exercised and shares were acquired before February 23, 1994.

Under the election that allows you to take advantage of unused capital gains exemption (described on page 107), you are deemed to have disposed of the property or properties on which you are making the election. If you are electing on CCPC shares that you acquired under a stock option plan, special rules apply that basically ensure that you are able to use the capital gains exemption election without having to currently recognize the employment benefit that would ordinarily arise if you actually sold the shares. The rules are complex and professional advice is highly recommended.

Gains on sales of stock in a qualifying small business corporation (QSBC) acquired by exercising options are still eligible for the enhanced $400,000 capital gains exemption. (When the expression "enhanced capital gains exemption" is discussed in this book, the amount of the exemption will be taken to be $400,000. This assumes that the general lifetime capital gains exemption has already been claimed. For individuals who have not used their $100,000 capital gains exemption in respect of other property, the enhanced exemption will be $500,000.)

When unexercised options under an employee stock option plan are held on the date of death of a taxpayer, an employment benefit equal to the difference between the fair market value of the options immediately before the employee's death and the amount paid by the employee to acquire the options will have to be included in the taxpayer's final income tax return.

Tax Tip 3

In general, decisions to invest or sell should be based on economic factors, with tax considerations secondary. However, in some cases clear tax advantages should be taken into account. For example, your shares of a CCPC acquired as a result of exercising a stock option prior to May 23, 1985 should be sold before selling your other securities. There will be no taxable benefit and the full gain is a capital gain. Although the $100,000 lifetime capital gains exemption has been eliminated, there may still be opportunities to shelter capital gains with unused capital gains exemption in 1995 and 1996 (see page 107); gains realized on the disposition of QSBC shares remain eligible for the enhanced capital gains exemption.

Tax Tip 4

If you borrow to finance the purchase of shares when exercising stock options, the interest expense on the loan is tax deductible. The interest expense will, however, be added to your cumulative net investment losses (see page 115).

Frequent flyer points

If you accumulate frequent flyer credits while travelling on business trips paid for by your employer and then use the points for yourself or your family for personal air travel, Revenue Canada requires you to determine and include in your income the fair market value of any benefits enjoyed. If your employer did not control the program, it is your responsibility to calculate and report the benefit.

28   Taxable benefits and the GST

Although salaries, wages, commissions and other remuneration paid to employees are not subject to the Goods and Services Tax (GST), fringe benefits or perks may be. Some of the more common perks that are included in your income as taxable benefits and that are subject to GST are:

- the benefit from personal use of your employer's automobile;

- short-term board and lodging (less than one month);

- the cost of tools, certain gifts, and frequent flyer programs;

- tuition fees for GST-taxable courses; and

- non-cash incentives such as prizes, awards and holiday trips that are GST-taxable in the marketplace and that are provided as benefits to employees.

GST will not apply to prizes or awards given to employees in the form of cash or a cheque.

Employers who are not registered for GST generally do not have to remit the GST on employee benefits. However, the GST element of taxable employee benefits must still be included in an employee's income for tax purposes.

Nontaxable benefits

Many employees receive other forms of compensation as well as those discussed already. Known as fringe benefits or perquisites ("perks" for short), a dwindling number of these non-cash benefits are received tax-free. Here are some examples:

- employer contributions to registered pension and deferred profit sharing plans (within limits);

- reimbursement of moving expenses;

- employee counselling services (including tobacco, drug or alcohol counselling, stress management counselling and job placement and retirement counselling) provided by or paid for by the employer;

- tuition fees for courses taken for the employer's benefit;

- employee discounts (within limits);

- subsidized meals, provided the employee is required to pay a reasonable charge;

- distinctive uniforms and special clothing (including safety footwear);

- use of employer's recreational facilities (except board and lodging at a vacation property such as a summer hotel or hunting lodge);

- social or athletic club memberships, but only if the membership is advantageous to the employer;

- reimbursement of a loss on the sale of a home due to an employment transfer;

- reasonable allowances for taxi fares, "para-transport" and parking provided to employees who are eligible for the disability tax credit by reason of a severe and prolonged impairment of mobility or sight; and

- allowances for attendant care required to enable an employee who qualifies for the disability tax credit to perform employment duties.

Employee relocation reimbursements

A job transfer could require you to move from one city to another within the same province, or across the country. Depending on the location and timing of a move, an employee could incur significant additional costs to acquire a home comparable to the one left behind. As part of an employment package, many employers compensate employees for higher housing prices in the new work location.

A number of court decisions dealt with payments of various types to employees in partial reimbursement of increased costs in new locations. In one case, the Federal Court of Appeal overturned the decisions of the lower courts and found that the taxpayer had to include the payments received from his employer in his employment income as a taxable benefit. The facts in another case, currently under appeal, are quite similar.

Essentially, a distinction was made between relocation payments that compensate employees for increased housing costs in a new location and for losses suffered on the sale of a previous home. The case affirms the taxability of payments for relocating to a more expensive location and the exemption from tax of relocation payments that reimburse an employee for actual losses incurred on a sale.

The recent case law has significantly narrowed the scope for providing employees with tax-free relocation payments. Indeed, a payment must meet all of the following criteria to be considered a non-taxable benefit:

- the payment must reimburse actual expenses or losses that are a direct consequence of a change in the employee's place of residence due to a change in work site;

- the payment results in no economic benefit to the employee;

- the payment is a reimbursement of an actual, quantifiable loss or expense, not merely an allowance or reimbursement of a general economic loss; and

- the payment is made to reimburse an expense incurred in respect of, in the course of, or by virtue of, the taxpayer's employment.

Other than home loss reimbursements and mortgage interest differential payments, the government has not acknowledged the tax-free status of any other type of relocation payment and each arrangement must be evaluated on its own merits. Further, the jurisprudence does not provide support for excluding from an employee's income employer relocation payments directed at defraying higher costs at a new work location, such as amounts paid as housing subsidies, cost-of-living differentials and reimbursements of excess tax costs.

If you would like to read (or bring to the attention of your professional advisor) some of the higher-level court decisions that dealt with employee relocation payments and that are the basis of the foregoing criteria, here are some of the more important case citations: *Cyril John Ransom v. Minister of National Revenue*, 67 DTC 5235 (Ex.Ct.); *Her Majesty the Queen v. Vincent Lao*, 93 DTC 5251 (FCTD); *Attorney General of Canada v. Roland M. MacDonald*, 94 DTC 6262 (FCA); *Her Majesty the Queen v. William R. Phillips*, 94 DTC 6177 (FCA).

Tax Tip 5

If, as a result of a job transfer, you received a relocation payment in a prior year that is not statute-barred and you excluded the amount from income, you should reconsider the circumstances to determine whether the exclusion is still justified. It would be prudent to discuss your situation with your professional advisor.

Tax Tip 6

If you will be relocating in the near future, consider suggesting that your employer review, and possibly restructure, the company's relocation program to ensure the most effective tax treatment. For example, although payments for defraying higher costs at a new work location, including payments for the incremental interest cost of assuming a new mortgage with both a higher interest rate and a higher principal amount, appear to be taxable, the reimbursement of increased mortgage interest payments resulting from an employer-initiated move may not be.

32 | Employment deductions

The Income Tax Act is not generous in permitting deductions in the computation of employment income. Only those expenses specifically included in a short list are deductible. Some of those with more general application are discussed below.

Moving expenses

Eligible moving expenses incurred in connection with beginning employment or full-time postsecondary education at a new location in Canada are deductible if your new residence is at least 40 kilometres closer to your new work or school location and if the expenses are not reimbursed by your employer. Eligible expenses are deductible only from income earned at the new location. Amounts not deducted in one year may be carried forward to the next year.

Eligible moving expenses include travelling costs for you and your family, including a reasonable amount for meals and lodging; moving and storage costs for your household effects; the costs of cancelling a lease or selling the old home; and legal costs of purchasing a new home.

A reimbursement of reasonable moving costs by your employer is not considered a taxable benefit. On the other hand, you cannot deduct costs that the employer reimburses.

Although taxes imposed on the transfer or registration of title to a new residence are eligible moving expenses (as long as you are selling an old one), changes to the rules clarify that the GST related to the purchase of a new residence is not included in the definition of taxes eligible for deduction.

Tax Tip 7

Since provincial tax is based on your province of residence on December 31, a higher than expected tax liability may arise with a move to another jurisdiction. If this will be the case, consider postponing your move until after the year end. On the other hand, consider accelerating the move if you are moving to a province with a lower tax rate.

Legal expenses

You may deduct legal costs paid to collect salary or wages from your employer or former employer. Legal expenses paid to collect or establish a right to a retiring allowance or pension benefit are deductible within a seven-year carryforward period in computing income for the year in which the allowance or benefit is received. The deduction is limited to the amount of retiring allowance or pension benefits you received, less any portion that has been transferred to an RPP or RRSP.

Tax Tip 8

If you incurred legal costs to collect pension income in the last three years, consider asking Revenue Canada to reassess your return for the period in question. Your tax refund could be significant.

Child care expenses

Working parents may deduct the cost of child care within specific limits. In most cases, the deduction must be claimed by the lower income spouse.

The maximum child care deduction depends on the child's age and any infirmity, as the table shows.

The maximum deduction is $5,000 for each child who is under seven years of age at the end of the year or has a severe or prolonged mental or physical impairment for which a Disability Credit Certificate

34   has been submitted. The deduction is $3,000 for each child who is less than 15 years of age at the end of the year or who is not eligible for the $5,000 deduction but has a mental or physical infirmity and is dependent.

Child care expense: maximum deductions

			Child's age (at December 31)		
			15 or more	7 to 14	Under 7
	No Infirmity				
Mental or physical infirmity	Infirmity does not qualify for the $5,000 maximum deduction	Child not dependent on taxpayer or taxpayer's spouse	None		
		Child is dependent on taxpayer or taxpayer's spouse		$3,000	
	Severe and prolonged impairment, for which a Disability Credit Certificate has been submitted			$5,000	

Eligible costs include day-care or babysitting, boarding school and camp expenses. Medical expenses, tuition, clothing or trans-portation expenses are not eligible for this deduction.

Tax Tip 9

For child care payments to be deductible in respect of the cur-rent year, they must be made by December 31. If you make January's payment in December, however, you are not permitted to deduct the amount until the following year.

Contributions to RPPs, RRSPs, DPSPs

Employees often accumulate funds to provide future retirement benefits through tax deductible contributions to a registered pension plan (RPP), a registered retirement savings plan (RRSP), a deferred profit sharing plan (DPSP) or some combination of these plans.

Once more with feeling! The rules dealing with contribution limits for tax assisted retirement savings are being modified yet again. Proposals in the 1995 federal budget will both reduce and delay the phase-in of the maximum contribution limits. Refer to each section below — RPPs, RRSPs and DPSPs — to see how the changes will affect you.

The rules that govern tax assistance for saving in pension and retirement savings plans are intended to ensure that individuals are treated equally, whether they save through RPPs, RRSPs or DPSPs.

Although the rules are fairly straightforward if you save for your retirement solely through RRSPs, they can be complicated if you are a member of an RPP or a DPSP. The Pension Adjustment (see below) determines what portion, if any, of the maximum RRSP contribution is replaced by benefits accrued under an RPP or a DPSP. The maximum amount you can contribute to your RRSP must then be reduced accordingly.

• Pension Adjustment (PA)

Simply put, your Pension Adjustment (PA) measures the benefits accrued to you as a member of a pension plan. The maximum you will be allowed to contribute to an RRSP is reduced by your PA.

The following table shows how the PA calculation depends on the type of pension plan:

The PA (pension adjustment) calculation

	Type of plan		
	DPSP	**RPP**	**No pension**
	Money purchase	**Defined benefit**	
PA	Total employee and employer contributions in the year (generally)	Complex calculation intended to measure value of benefits accrued in the year	None

In a money purchase plan, the pension you receive depends on the investment earnings of the pension fund. In a defined benefit plan, pension payments are independent of the fund's earnings,

36   depending instead on a formula that usually involves a percentage of your average earnings and your period of pensionable employment.

Your employer is responsible for determining your PA. Your T4 slip for 1994 employment earnings will tell the amount of your PA. You will have to reduce your RRSP limit by the prior year's PA. Revenue Canada will also advise you of your 1995 RRSP deduction limit on your 1994 Notice of Assessment or late in 1995.

If you are a member of a foreign pension plan, you may still have a PA. For example, if you are resident in Canada, but work primarily outside Canada, you may be required to calculate your own PA-like amount with respect to any foreign plan to which you belong. In other circumstances, it will be your employer's responsibility to calculate and report your PA. The PA calculations can be very complex. If you are concerned about whether your PA has been calculated and reported correctly, consider having your tax advisor discuss the matter with your employer.

To complicate matters further, something called a Past Service Pension Adjustment (PSPA) may result if, for example, your pension plan is retroactively upgraded to provide better benefits or if you transfer benefits to a new plan and purchase additional past service benefits. If you have a PSPA, the amount that you may contribute to your RRSP will require adjustment. Once again, the onus is on your employer to provide you with the necessary information regarding these very complicated rules.

RRSP contribution limits may be reduced by your PA and PSPA

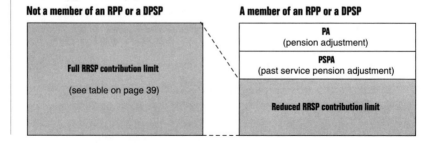

Not a member of an RPP or a DPSP	A member of an RPP or a DPSP
Full RRSP contribution limit (see table on page 39)	**PA** (pension adjustment) / **PSPA** (past service pension adjustment) / **Reduced RRSP contribution limit**

• Registered pension plans (RPPs) – money purchase

If you belong to a money purchase RPP, you may make a tax-deductible contribution to your plan in 1995 equal to 18% of your 1994 employment income, to a maximum of $15,500, minus the contribution your employer makes to your plan (see the table on page 39). You reach the $15,500 maximum when your employment earnings are $86,111.

The 1995 federal budget proposes to reduce the money purchase limit to $13,500 in 1996. The limit will then increase by $1,000 to $14,500 for 1997 and a further $1,000 to $15,500 in 1998. The limit of $15,500 will be indexed by growth in the average industrial wage in Canada after 1998.

• Registered pension plans (RPPs) – defined benefit

Generally, the amount you may contribute to a defined benefit RPP and deduct for tax purposes is not limited, as long as the contributions are in respect of current service and are required under the provisions of the plan. However, the government caps the amount of pension an individual may receive, and the provisions of your RPP will ensure that the restrictions are met by limiting how much you and your employer can contribute. Maximum contributions relate to the maximum benefit that can be accrued, which in turn is based on a maximum annual pension allowed in the first year of retirement. That maximum pension equals your years of pensionable service, multiplied by the lesser of:

- 2% of the average of the best three consecutive years of salary; and

- $1,722 (the 1995 federal budget proposes to freeze this limit until 1999 when it will be increased in accordance with changes to the average industrial wage).

As the graph on the following page shows, the $1,722 cap corresponds to an average of $86,111 for the best three consecutive years of salary.

Maximum pension (per year of pensionable service)

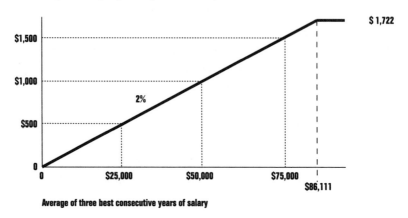

Average of three best consecutive years of salary

• **Registered pension plans – additional voluntary contributions (AVCs)**

AVCs are contributions made under a money purchase provision of an RPP that are not required as a general condition of membership under the plan. Even in a defined benefit RPP, AVCs generally provide benefits on a money purchase basis. (However, if voluntary contributions are made to purchase defined benefits, the PSPA rules discussed earlier must be considered). AVCs are permitted as long as the Pension Adjustment limits (see page 35) are not exceeded.

Prior to October 9, 1986, past service AVCs could be made under certain circumstances. If this type of AVCs were made, have not been deducted and were annuitized as retirement income, up to $3,500 a year may be deducted against post-1986 retirement income.

• **Registered retirement savings plans (RRSPs)**

An RRSP is a tax-deferred investment vehicle that allows you to invest money now, with a view to using the accumulated funds as retirement income commencing not later than the end of the year in which you turn 71. Your contributions are tax deductible within specified limits. If you borrow money to make an RRSP contribution, the interest payments are not tax deductible.

		RRSP	DPSP	RPP	
		(Limits to be reduced by the PA and PSPA for members of RPPs or DPSPs)	(Employer's contributions only)	**Money purchase** (Limits apply to total employer and employee contributions)	**Defined benefit**
Fixed dollar limit*	**1995**	$14,500 (if income > $80,556)	$7,750 (if income > $43,056)	$15,500 (if income > $86,111)	**No direct limit** (Contributions governed by actuarial principles and specific rules.)
	1996	$13,500 (if income > $75,000*)	$6,750 (if income > $37,500*)	$13,500 (if income > $75,000*)	
	1997	$13,500 (if income > $75,000*)	$7,250 (if income > $40,278*)	$14,500 (if income > $80,556*)	
	1998	$14,500 (if income > $80,556*)	$7,750 (if income > $43,056*)	$15,500 (if income > $86,111*)	
	1999	$15,500 (if income > $86,111*)	Indexed		
	After 1999				
Income-based limit (all years)		18% of previous year's earned income	18% of employment income		

* Below the given level of income, the 18% limit applies rather than the fixed dollar limit.

As the table above shows, your RRSP contributions for 1995 cannot exceed 18% of your earned income for the previous year, up to a dollar limit of $14,500 (which corresponds to $80,556 of earned income). If you are a member of an RPP or a DPSP, these limits are reduced by your:

• pension adjustment (PA) for the previous year, described on page 35; and

• past service pension adjustment (PSPA), described on page 36.

The 1995 federal budget proposes to reduce the RRSP contribution limit to $13,500 in 1996. The limit will remain at $13,500 for 1997, then increase by $1,000 for each of 1998 and 1999 when the maximum will reach $15,500. The limit of $15,500 will be indexed by growth in the average industrial wage in Canada after 1999.

To be deductible in a particular year, your RRSP contributions must be made before the end of the year or in the first 60 days of the following year. Beginning in 1991, if you do not make the full RRSP contribution that you are entitled to, the balance can be contributed and deducted for income tax purposes without limitation over a period of at least seven years (including the year to which the unused RRSP contribution room relates). The amount of unused RRSP contribution room that can be carried beyond the seven years is restricted.

Remember that earned income does not include any type of periodic retirement or pension payment or benefit, including retiring allowances, death benefits and amounts received from an RRSP. In addition to your regular RRSP contribution, you may be able to transfer a portion of a retiring allowance to your RRSP. The 1995 federal budget proposes to phase-out tax-free rollovers to RRSPs. You may, however, continue to transfer up to $2,000 per year of service before 1996, plus $1,500 per year of service before 1989 during which you were not a member of an RPP or DPSP.

• Self-directed RRSPs

Funds in your RRSP may be invested in a number of ways. If you choose to establish your RRSP at a financial institution such as a bank, trust company or life insurance company, you will probably have a deposit account with investments such as term deposits or Guaranteed Investment Certificates (GICs).

You may also choose to have a self-directed RRSP. This option is somewhat riskier and takes more time and effort on your part than a simple deposit account. Ordinarily, you will set up a self-directed RRSP through a financial institution or your broker.

There are restrictions on the types of investments your RRSP may hold. Some of the more popular qualified investments include: cash, shares or bonds of corporations listed on Canadian stock exchanges, T-Bills, GICs, government bonds, mutual funds, and certain small business shares. Further, up to 20 percent of your portfolio may be invested in foreign assets. If the total cost amount of the foreign property held exceeds the 20 percent limitation, the excess will generally be subject to a significant penalty tax.

Technical changes dealing with the foreign property limit were introduced in July 1995. The definition of foreign property is to be amended so that shares and debts issued by a Canadian corporation are not considered as foreign property if the Canadian corporation has a substantial presence in Canada. The proposals also provide that, subject to the substantial Canadian presence exemption, shares and debt issued by a Canadian corporation will be considered to be foreign property if the shares issued by the corporation derive their value primarily from any foreign property — not merely portfolio investments in foreign property.

• Spousal RRSP contributions

Contributions to a spousal RRSP based on your contribution limit are deductible from your income. These contributions, however, reduce the amount you can contribute to your own plan for the year.

You can continue to contribute to your spouse's RRSP until he or she is 71, even if you have already reached that age. In addition to gaining access to the pension income credit, receipts from a spousal RRSP may help equalize the amount of retirement income you both receive, and may place you in a lower tax bracket.

Tax Tip 10

Don't get trapped by a timing rule associated with withdrawals from a spousal RRSP. If you withdraw amounts from a spousal RRSP, you, rather than your spouse, will have to include the withdrawals in your income to the extent that you paid the tax-deductible premiums into the spousal plan in the year or in the immediately preceding two taxation years. Many people make the mistake of thinking of RRSP contributions as having been made in the year they are deductible, rather than in the year they were actually made. For example, a contribution made in February 1995 and deducted on your 1994 tax return will be included in your income and taxed on your return if the amounts are withdrawn before 1998, i.e., within two years of the time when the contribution was made.

42 • Over-contributions to an RRSP

As discussed on page 38, if you contribute to an RRSP, you need to be concerned with the maximum amount of RRSP contributions that you may deduct for tax purposes for a particular year. You also need to ensure that you do not incur a penalty tax because you have overcontributed to your RRSP. Up until recently, you would not incur penalties unless you exceeded your RRSP contribution limit by more than $8,000. Rather than viewing this allowance as protective cushion against inadvertent or unavoidable overcontributions, the government was of the view that too many taxpayers took the opportunity to put additional, albeit non-deductible, monies into their RRSPs. The 1995 federal budget proposes to remedy this perceived abuse by reducing the overcontribution allowance to $2,000, effective January 1, 1996. The measure will be phased-in to allow existing excess contributions to be retained until they can be drawn down and deducted against new RRSP room, rather than forcing them to be withdrawn. If you had an overcontribution greater than $2,000 on February 27, 1995, you will be required to apply the contributions against your unused RRSP room beginning in 1996. (There is no transitional amount for individuals who had not attained 18 years of age before 1995.)

For example, assume that you have made maximum RRSP contributions over the last few years. You are fully up to date, including maximum contributions for 1994 made by the end of that year. You contributed $22,500 to your RRSP at the beginning of February 1995: the maximum $14,500 for 1995, plus $8,000 of overcontribution. If your deduction limit for 1996 is $13,500, you will have to treat $6,000 of your overcontribution as a deductible contribution for 1996 and will be able to contribute only a further $7,500. Of course, you will be able to deduct $13,500 on your 1996 tax return. You should not incur any penalty tax since your overcontribution will not exceed $2,000.

The proposed rules also provide an additional margin for certain group RRSP contributions and defer the effect of past service pension adjustments.

The amendment dealing with group RRSPs ensures that, within limits, non-discretionary contributions can be made to a group RRSP on the basis of current year earnings without being caught by the penalty tax.

The new rules also provide that a PSPA will not cause RRSP contributions to become subject to the penalty tax in the year in which the PSPA arises. PSPAs, however, reduce the unused RRSP deduction room that is carried forward and are therefore taken into account for penalty tax purposes in subsequent years.

The penalty is 1% per month of your "cumulative excess amount" (the amount of the over-contribution above $2,000) at the end of the month. The $2,000 over-contribution threshold is not available if you are under the age of nineteen.

If you over-contribute (perhaps because of lower-than-expected earned income), you may end up paying double tax, i.e., you don't get a deduction for tax purposes for the excess amount and you will pay tax on the amount when it is eventually withdrawn as retirement income. You can, however, avoid paying double tax: when you receive your Notice of Assessment for the year in which the excess arose, you may withdraw that excess amount tax-free, in:

- the year of the over-contribution;

- the year you receive the assessment; or

- the year immediately following either of those years.

If the over-contribution is intentional, you lose the ability to make a tax-free withdrawal.

Even though you have this opportunity to withdraw the excess amount tax-free, you will still be liable for the penalty tax if the over-contribution exceeds $2,000. If your over-contribution was due to a reasonable error, you can ask Revenue Canada to waive the penalty tax.

• Deferred profit sharing plans (DPSPs)

A deferred profit sharing plan (DPSP) can be used in lieu of an RPP.

44   A DPSP is an arrangement under which an employer makes payments — for example, a percentage of annual profits — to a trustee. (Employee contributions, although no longer allowed, were permitted prior to 1991.)

The trustee holds and invests the contributions for the benefit of employees who are plan members.

Tax-deductible contributions may be made to a DPSP by your employer. As the table on page 39 shows, the contribution for 1995 is limited to the lesser of 18% of your remuneration and $7,750. As discussed in the section dealing with money purchase RPPs, the federal budget proposes to reduce the money purchase contribution limits after 1995. Contributions to a DPSP continue to be limited to one-half the money purchase limit. Accordingly, the contribution limits to a DPSP will be as follows: $6,750 in 1996; $7,250 in 1997; and $7,750 in 1998. The limit of $7,750 will be indexed by growth in the average industrial wage in Canada after 1998. Employee contributions to DPSPs are not permitted.

Amounts withdrawn from a DPSP are taxable, but in determining the taxable amount, you may deduct the contributions that you made to the plan (which were permitted before 1991).

You may transfer lump sum proceeds from a DPSP into an RPP, an RRSP, or another DPSP, generally tax-free.

• Individual pension plans (IPPs)

An important objective of the sweeping changes to the rules governing tax assistance for retirement savings was equality between RPPs and RRSPs. That goal, however, could not be fully realized. For example, a well-designed defined benefit RPP can, in certain circumstances, provide greater tax-assistance than an RRSP.

To allow taxpayers to take advantage of this opportunity the Individual Pension Plan (IPP) was developed by Price Waterhouse. An IPP is essentially a defined benefit RPP that is specifically designed to provide the maximum benefits that can be funded prior to retirement. As the name suggests, each IPP has only one member, which permits flexibility to meet each individual's circumstances. The IPP also shares similarities with defined contribution arrangements, such as RRSPs, in that all funds in the plan belong to the member and will be used to provide benefits to the member or heirs. The IPP is a feasible option for an individual who is over the age of 38, earns at least $87,000 in 1995 and expects earnings to grow at least as fast as the average industrial wage.

As a result of proposed changes to the pension and RRSP limits announced in the federal budget, contributions to an IPP will be reduced. The relative advantages of an IPP over an RRSP, however, will remain unchanged.

This is a complex area and professional advice is a must. You will need competent assistance to assess the potential benefits of a plan to you, and, if an IPP is indeed appropriate to your particular circumstances, to establish the IPP itself.

• Locked-in RRSPs

The 1995 federal budget contains proposals that will allow holders of RRSPs that are locked in under a provision of the *Pension Benefits Standards Act* to purchase Life Income Funds. This alternative affords individuals a more flexible way of managing retirement income funds. Currently, you may only purchase life annuities with funds in locked-in RRSPs.

Other expenses

Annual dues required to be paid to a professional body, a trade union or similar body are generally deductible. Office rent, salary paid to an assistant, and the cost of supplies that an employee is required to pay under an employment contract may also be deductible.

If your office is part of a house or apartment that you rent, you may be able to deduct certain home office expenses, as the table shows, as long as the required conditions are met.

46 | **Home office expenses – employees**

Deductible (if conditions are satisfied*)	Not deductible
Rent and maintenance attributable to the office. Maintenance expenses include: – fuel – light bulbs – electricity – minor repairs – cleaning materials	– capital cost allowance – mortgage interest
Commissioned sales people only may deduct a portion of these expenses: – taxes – insurance	

* Expenses are deductible only if the workplace is:
• your principal place of employment; **or**
• used by you both:
  – exclusively for the purpose of earning employment income; **and**
  – "on a regular and continuous basis" for meeting customers or other persons in the course of employment.

Home office expenses can be deducted only up to the amount of your employment income for the year. To the extent that you cannot use the full deduction in a particular year, you may carry forward work space expenses indefinitely and deduct them from employment income in future years.

Reduced employee withholdings

(See page 205 — Interest-free loans to the government?)

Tax Tip 11

If your taxable income will be substantially less than the amount your employer uses to calculate the tax to withhold, possibly as a result of extraordinary deductible expenses that you have incurred, write to your district taxation office requesting a reduction. (You may want to discuss this with your professional advisor first.)

Employees and automobiles

The taxation of automobile benefits and expenses has always been complex. If you own your car, reasonable distance-based allowances for your costs will not be included in your income; other allowances may be. If you received a taxable allowance, you may be able to deduct some of the actual expenses you incurred.

Automobiles – taxable benefits

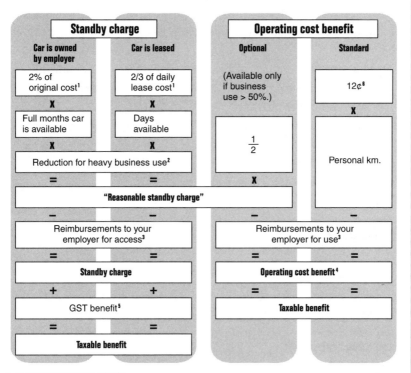

Standby charge		Operating cost benefit	
Car is owned by employer	**Car is leased**	**Optional**	**Standard**
2% of original cost[1]	2/3 of daily lease cost[1]	(Available only if business use > 50%.)	12¢[6]
X	**X**		**X**
Full months car is available	Days available	$\frac{1}{2}$	Personal km.
X	**X**		
Reduction for heavy business use[2]		**X**	
=	**=**		
"Reasonable standby charge"			
–	**–**	**–**	**–**
Reimbursements to your employer for access[3]		Reimbursements to your employer for use[3]	
=	**=**	**=**	**=**
Standby charge		**Operating cost benefit**[4]	
+	**+**	**=**	**=**
GST benefit[5]		**Taxable benefit**	
=	**=**		
Taxable benefit			

1 Costs include PST, but not GST.

2 Reduction factor $= \dfrac{\text{personal kilometres}}{1{,}000 \text{ kilometres x full months car is available}}$

   (Available only if business use is at least 90% and personal kilometres average less than 1,000 per month.)

3 Any operating costs reimbursed to your employer must be paid within 45 days after the end of the year. Standby charges must be paid in the year.

4 Considered to already include a GST benefit component.

5 7% of "reasonable standby charge" recalculated excluding PST in original purchase cost or daily lease cost.

6 9¢ for employees whose principal source of employment is selling or leasing automobiles.

48   If your employer provides you with an automobile (as defined in the Income Tax Act), you are considered to have received two types of taxable benefits: a standby charge (which reflects your access to the car) and an operating cost benefit (which reflects the personal portion of such expenses that are paid for by your employer).

If your employer provides you with a motor vehicle that is not an automobile, you are still considered to have received taxable benefits (i.e., a personal use benefit and an operating cost benefit), but these benefits are calculated differently than the benefits described below.

The standby charge is calculated differently depending on whether the employer owns the car or the car is leased, as the first two columns of the chart on page 47 indicate.

For purposes of calculating the standby charge, original cost and lease payments do not include the GST, but do include provincial sales taxes. See page 49 for an explanation of how the GST does affect taxable benefits relating to automobiles.

Tax Tip 12

The standby charge is calculated on the original cost of the car and does not decrease as the value of the car declines with age. After a few years, it may be cheaper to eliminate the standby charge by buying the car from your employer.

• Operating cost benefit

The federal operating cost benefit formula is simply 12¢ × total personal kilometres (as shown in the chart on page 47). The 12¢ per kilometre rate will be reduced to 9¢ per kilometre for employees whose principal source of employment is selling or leasing automobiles. The reduced rate applies to 1994 and subsequent taxation years.

Alternatively, if you use the car more than 50% for employment purposes, you can elect to calculate the benefit as half of the standby charge, less any amounts you reimbursed to your employer.

The operating cost benefit is considered to already include a GST component.

Tax Tip 13

If your personal use is less than 50% of the total use and you prefer the alternative operating cost benefit calculation, you must notify your employer in writing before the end of the year.

Tax Tip 14

Minimize your personal use of an employer-provided automobile to reduce your operating cost benefit, and in some cases your standby charge benefit. There may be an advantage if you use your own car for personal purposes.

Tax Tip 15

Reimburse your employer for all personal use operating expenses within 45 days after the year-end (i.e., by February 14) to eliminate your operating cost benefit. In particular, if your employer has paid only a small portion of the operating expenses, consider repaying these amounts before the February 14 deadline so that you will not have a taxable benefit of 12¢ per personal-use kilometre for the entire year.

Tax planning measures may be available to reduce or avoid your operating cost benefit. Your arrangements should be evaluated to identify tax planning opportunities for reducing the benefit.

• Employer-provided automobiles and the GST

If your employer owns the car you use for business purposes, you must include in your income a standby charge based on the actual cost of the automobile, including provincial sales tax (PST). In addition, your taxable benefit in respect of the automobile must reflect the GST that relates to that portion of the purchase cost.

For example, the table below shows how the total standby charge that is added to your T4 slip includes $420 to reflect the GST component.

Standby charge in respect of:	employer's $25,000 car	($25,000 + $2,000 PST*) x 2% x 12 months = $6,480
	GST	25,000 x 2% x 12 months x 7% = $420
Total standby charge		$6,900

* Provincial sales tax (PST) is assumed to be 8% for this example.

Note: The GST component must be added to the standby charge even if your employer did not pay GST on the purchase or lease cost of the vehicle.

The same applies to the standby charge for an automobile that is leased: the taxable benefit on a leased automobile must reflect two-thirds of the GST that would be applicable to the lease cost.

The amount of any operating cost benefit for an automobile already reflects an estimate of the GST your employer has paid on personal operating expenses.

For purposes of calculating the GST portion of the standby charge benefit, any reimbursement payment that you made to your employer in respect of the benefit is not to be taken into account.

Employee automobile expenses

If you use your own car in carrying out your employment duties, you will have a number of decisions to make. You will have to determine whether any amount you receive from your employer constitutes a reimbursement or an allowance; the tax consequences are different. You will then have to determine whether you are entitled to deduct any car expenses, and then how much.

• Reimbursements

A reimbursement is an amount that you receive from your employer to repay you for amounts (including GST) that you spent on your employer's business. Generally, you do not have to pay tax on a reimbursement unless it is a payment for personal expenses. An allowance, on the other hand, is a payment that you receive from your employer in addition to your salary and wages and that you need not account for. Although the rules dealing with whether or not an allowance has to be included in your income are quite specific, some latitude is nonetheless permitted in applying them.

• Allowances

Essentially, an allowance must be reasonable for it not to be considered taxable to an employee. An automobile allowance is considered reasonable only if it is computed using an appropriate per kilometre rate that is applied to business driving by an employee. If you receive an allowance from your employer that is solely distance-based, it will ordinarily be considered to be reasonable and would not be taxable to you. Accordingly, your employer would not be required to withhold tax in respect of the allowance paid.

If the allowance is determined on another basis, it will not be considered to be reasonable and, therefore, will be taxable to you and subject to withholding at source. A taxable car allowance is not subject to GST. Since the allowance is included in your income, you may be able to claim reasonable business-related expenses.

If the allowance is distance-based and would otherwise be considered to be reasonable, but you believe that the allowance you receive is not reasonable because your business-related expenses exceed the amount of the allowance, you may choose to add the allowance to your income and claim reasonable business-related expenses. The onus is on you, however, to make this decision.

• Deducting automobile expenses

What's the bottom line? You may be permitted to deduct reasonable automobile expenses that you are required to incur in travelling to carry out your employment duties, so long as you are not reimbursed for the expenses and your employer does not pay you an automobile travelling allowance that was excluded from your income. You may deduct a portion of operating expenses, prorated according to the proportion that the distance driven in the course of employment is of the total distance driven. You are also entitled to a prorated portion of capital cost allowance (CCA), as well as leasing costs or interest on funds borrowed to buy the car, subject to certain limits.

If you deduct business-related car expenses on your personal tax return and your employer is a GST registrant, you may be eligible to apply for a rebate of the GST you paid. The rebate is not available if you choose to include an otherwise reasonable tax-free allowance in your income in order to claim business-related expenses.

	Maximum deduction*
Capital cost allowance (CCA) base	$24,000**
Monthly interest charges	$300
Monthly lease payments***	$650**

* For automobiles acquired or leases entered into after August 1989.

** Plus GST and PST on $24,000 and $650

*** Or lesser amount (determined by formula) for certain luxury vehicles.

Tax Tip 16

If you have two cars, consider using one exclusively for business and the other for personal use, to simplify record keeping.

Loss of employment

In today's weak economic environment, loss of employment seems to be more of a risk than ever.

In a plant closure, which may take place over a period of months or even a year or more, employees may be in a position to plan for coping with expenses, to re-arrange payment schedules for recurring obligations such as mortgages, and to seek other employment without urgency. When termination is unanticipated, however, perhaps because of downsizing or the takeover of an employer by another corporation, employees may find themselves in a difficult predicament, with the need to act quickly.

Little anyone does or says can mitigate the effect of loss of employment. There are, however, things you should be aware of and that you should consider in the unfortunate event that you find yourself without work.

Working with your employer is the first step in the process. Although keeping costs down is a major concern, many of today's more enlightened employers are also concerned with providing employees with tax-effective severance arrangements that do not result in an additional burden to the employer.

Sitting down with your spouse (and possibly other family members) and preparing a realistic budget and cash flow schedule is another critical element in this process. You need to determine exactly how much money you expect to be coming in and for how long, what your expenses are, which expenses you can defer and which you can cut entirely. If you anticipate a prolonged period of unemployment, don't wait until a major payment is due to the bank, for example, to let them know that you are unemployed. Schedule an appointment with your banker as soon as possible and try to re-arrange your payment terms.

Your re-employment counsellor (see below) should also be able to give you some suggestions on how to manage your financial position while you are looking for work.

The severance package

• Retiring allowances

The term "retiring allowance" may be a little deceptive because the

54   definition encompasses a wide range of payments. A retiring allowance is an amount that you receive upon or after retirement from an office or employment in recognition of long service; or an amount in respect of a loss of an office or employment whether or not it was received on account or in lieu of payment of damages, or pursuant to a court order or judgment.

Your severance package may be determined by reference to your current remuneration, including benefits. Although this may seem logical, the way in which your "golden parachute" is structured may prohibit you from making special tax-effective transfers to your RRSP or RPP (see below). Even though you no longer actually report for work, your severance arrangement may provide that in addition to amounts paid to you on termination, certain benefits of employment (medical and dental plan benefits and insurance coverage, for example) will also continue for a specified period. Because of the continuation of benefits, Revenue Canada may consider the payments you receive from your former employer to be employment income and not retiring allowances. Consequently, you may not be eligible to transfer these amounts to your RRSP or RPP.

• Transfer to RRSP or RPP

The 1995 federal budget proposes to phase out the provisions allowing for the tax-free transfer of retiring allowances to an RRSP after 1995. You may, however, continue to transfer up to $2,000 per year of service before 1996. There is no change to the rule that allows you to transfer up to $1,500 per year of service before 1989 in which you did not have a vested interest in contributions made by employer to either a DPSP or an RPP.

Although transferring as much as you are able to your RRSP or RPP is a tax-effective strategy, you must also consider your cash flow requirements. If you anticipate a prolonged period of unemployment, you may need to reduce the amount of retiring allowance to be transferred to your RRSP or RPP.

• RPPs

If you participate in your employer's RPP, you will have to determine what choices you have regarding contributions that you and your employer have made to your plan. If you are over a specified age and/or have a certain number of years of service with your employer, you may not be able to access funds in your RPP because you are "locked-in". If that is the case, you may have to wait until you are eligible to receive a retirement pension out of the plan, or you may only be able to transfer the funds directly into a locked-in RRSP or, when you begin new employment, to your employer's RPP if that plan provides for such transfers.

If you are not locked-in to your RPP, you may transfer the funds to your RRSP. If this transfer is done directly, then you need not suffer any withholding tax. On the other hand, if you need the funds immediately, your employer will have to withhold tax from the amounts to be paid to you and you will also have to include the amounts in your income for tax purposes in the year you receive them. Of course, any tax withheld at source will be credited to you as a payment of tax.

You should contact your pension plan administrator for details about your plan and the options you have for the funds accumulated in the plan.

• Re-employment counselling/executive search services

As part of your severance package, your employer may provide you with executive search services or the services of a professional re-employment counsellor. Services of this nature that your employer either provides or pays for are not a taxable benefit to you.

Tax Tip 17

When negotiating your severance package, consider having your employer include re-employment counselling or executive search services. The counselling is generally very helpful, and the considerable cost that your employer would incur to provide you with the service is a tax-free benefit to you.

What if you disagree?

• Wrongful dismissal

The definition of retiring allowance is sufficiently broad to include damage awards made by a court in an action for wrongful dismissal. Accordingly, unless the facts indicate otherwise, an award for damages must be included in your income in the year you receive it.

Awards for damages to compensate for pain and suffering and mental distress may, however, be non-taxable receipts, depending on the facts and circumstances of the particular case. If you have sued your employer for wrongful dismissal and the court has awarded you damages, you should discuss the tax implications with your professional advisor.

• Legal expenses

You may generally deduct legal fees paid to collect or establish a right to salary or wages that are owed to you by your employer or former employer. Legal fees include amounts spent on negotiating your severance package as well as fees for litigation that becomes necessary.

Although amounts that you receive as retiring allowances are specifically excluded from the definition of salary and wages, you may deduct legal expenses associated with retiring allowances, but with a limitation. The deduction is limited to the amount of the retiring allowance actually received in the taxation year that you did not transfer to your RPP or RRSP. For example, if your retiring allowance is $20,000, you transfer $15,000 to an RRSP and your legal expenses are $6,000, you may deduct only $5,000 of legal expenses.

Retiring allowances may be paid over a period of time. Since legal expenses may be deducted only to the extent of retiring allowances that you actually receive, Revenue Canada permits you to deduct legal expenses that you incur to collect retiring allowances over a seven-year period. This means that you can deduct a portion of your legal expenses against the retiring allowances that you receive each year in the carryforward period.

Continuity of benefits

• Loss of disability, medical, dental benefits, etc.

Many employers provide attractive benefit packages such as dental benefits for the employee and his or her family members, medical and travel insurance and disability insurance. Although some severance packages may provide that these benefits continue for a short period after employment ceases, you should evaluate how you will replace these important elements of your compensation package and how much it will cost you to either get insurance coverage yourself, or to pay for services such as dental care out of your own pocket. Of course, if you have other employment lined up, this may not be a concern. If you anticipate a long period of unemployment, however, you should decide which types of expenses can be deferred and which services need to be replaced immediately.

Moving expenses

You may have to relocate to find new employment. If you move to a place in Canada that is at least 40 kilometres closer to your new work location than your old residence was you may claim eligible moving expenses, to the extent that they are not reimbursed to you by your new employer. You may deduct moving expenses only from income earned in your new capacity. If you move close to the end of the year, you may not have sufficient earnings against which to deduct moving expenses. In these circumstances, you may carry forward your moving expenses and deduct them the following year against income from your new employment.

58 | **Employees on temporary assignment**

Many employee moves are only temporary. Employees may be moved for various reasons: to a head office for a one or two-year assignment; to fill a temporarily vacant position; to open a new office; or even to carry out a short-term assignment in a desirable location as a perquisite. A temporary period can be anywhere from a few weeks or months to five years.

For income tax purposes, one of the most important issues for employees either coming into or leaving Canada on a temporary assignment is their residency status during the period. Residence is a question of fact; the term "resident" is not defined in the Canadian Income Tax Act. The courts have held that an individual is resident in Canada for tax purposes if Canada is the place where he or she, in the settled routine of life, regularly, normally or customarily lives.

Unless the circumstances suggest otherwise, an individual who is absent from Canada for two years or longer is generally considered a non-residency. Revenue Canada has recently been questioning the position taken by taxpayers who are out of the country for two or more years, but who have an intention to return. For example, employees on temporary assignment who are required under their employment contracts to return to Canada once their assignments are over. Revenue Canada has apparently accepted the non-residency status of such individuals, as long as all ties with Canada have clearly been severed during the non-residency period. There have been problems, however, when individuals have left homes in Canada that are vacant during their absence. Revenue Canada takes the position that residential ties with Canada have not been severed if a vacant home is available to the individual. Further, a home need not actually be vacant. A dwelling is generally considered to be available if it is leased to a related person, or to an unrelated person if less than three months' notice is required to terminate the lease.

Tax Tip 18

If you are planning to be out of the country on assignment for two or more years, ensure that you have in fact severed all ties with Canada. If you own a home and do not plan to sell it, you should consider renting it out to an unrelated person. The lease arrangement with the tenant should stipulate that a minimum of three months' notice is required for termination of the lease.

Although the two year rule is one that Revenue Canada generally applies, you may be able to successfully argue that you are a non-resident of Canada for a period of less than two years if the facts of the particular situation support that conclusion. For example, assume that you leave Canada to take up an assignment that you fully expect to extend beyond two years and you carefully sever all residential ties with Canada. Ten months into your contract, it is terminated for business reasons and you must return to Canada. The court found in favour of a taxpayer in a similar situation; the individual was found to have been a non-resident of Canada for a period less than two years.

Tax Tip 19

If you are going to be leaving Canada on a temporary assignment, discuss the situation with your professional advisor well in advance of your departure. There is a litany of steps you should take to ensure that you have in fact severed your ties with Canada. You do not want your tax planning strategies to fail because you neglected to take care of a few seemingly minor details that Revenue Canada might consider to preserve your ties with Canada.

An individual may be deemed to be a resident of Canada even though he or she is not actually a resident. Generally, this means that an individual is resident elsewhere. One of the most common types of deemed resident is a "sojourner". You are a sojourner if you are in Canada for periods totalling 183 days or more in a year. (The 183 figure comes from $365/2 = 182.5$.) If this is the case, you will be considered a resident of Canada for the whole year and will be taxed on your worldwide income. This rule is applied year by year. For example, suppose you live and work in Seattle. In 1995 you spend 192 days in Canada working on a project for your employer. While in Canada, you live in a hotel. You will be considered a deemed resident of Canada in 1995 and will be subject to tax on your worldwide income. In 1996, you continue working on your project, but spend only 110 days in Canada. In 1996, you will not be deemed to be a resident of Canada. You will, of course, be subject to Canadian tax on the income you earn performing employment duties in Canada.

A sojourner must be distinguished from an individual who actually takes up residence in Canada, whether or not the individual is present for 183 or more days in the year.

Canada has bilateral income tax treaties with many countries. When an individual appears to be a resident of Canada and another country, the treaties generally provide assistance through tie-breaker rules.

Depending on the circumstances, an individual's residency status and the time of taking up residence may be difficult to ascertain. A discussion with your professional tax advisor is strongly recommended well in advance of any move into or out of Canada.

In the comments below, it is assumed that employees temporarily in Canada are non-residents of Canada, and that employees on temporary assignment outside Canada remain Canadian residents throughout the period spent abroad.

Temporary assignments in Canada

If you are a non-resident of Canada, and you were employed in Canada at any time in the year or in a previous year, you will generally be subject to Canadian tax on your employment income and will be required to file a Canadian income tax return and a Québec income tax return if applicable. Depending on your country of residence, your employment income earned in Canada will probably be subject to tax in your home country as well.

The extent to which you will be able to obtain relief from double taxation will depend on whether or not foreign taxes are creditable against the income taxes levied under the laws of your country of residence, or whether there is a bilateral tax agreement between Canada and your home country.

The treaty rules regarding dependent personal services may provide relief from double taxation to individuals on international assignments. Generally, for remuneration received by individuals temporarily employed in Canada to be taxable in their home country only, the individuals must be present in Canada for less than 183 days and the remuneration must be paid by an employer that is neither a resident of Canada nor has a permanent establishment here. In addition, certain treaties set out a threshold amount of remuneration below which the host country (i.e., Canada) will not impose tax.

Temporary assignments outside Canada

The courts have held that everyone must be resident somewhere and that an individual can be resident in more than one place at the same time for tax purposes. If a resident of Canada goes abroad, but does not establish a permanent residence elsewhere, the presumption is that he or she remains a resident of Canada. Also, the fact that an individual establishes a permanent residence abroad does not by itself make the individual a non-resident of Canada. Where an individual is resident in Canada and, at the same time, resident in another country according to its laws, reference should be made to any tax convention or agreement that Canada may have with the other country.

A resident of Canada is taxed on his or her worldwide income. Accordingly, employment income earned during an assignment abroad will be subject to Canadian tax. The same income may, however, also be taxable in the foreign jurisdiction. Relief from double taxation will generally be available through either a tax treaty between Canada and the foreign country or the Canadian foreign tax credit provisions, or a combination of the two.

Tax Tip 20

If you are a Canadian resident during 1995 and have been or will be employed abroad for a period of more than six consecutive months that begins before the end of the year, you may be entitled to a tax credit designed to limit your Canadian tax liability. Generally, you must be employed by a Canadian resident, or a foreign affiliate of a Canadian resident, in connection with the exploration for or the exploitation of petroleum, natural gas, minerals or similar resources; or a construction, installation, agricultural or engineering activity. The credit, calculated annually, is determined by a formula that provides a tax reduction for overseas employment income that is less than $100,000.

Tax Tip 21

If you are considering a temporary assignment, and your employer has a tax protection or a tax equalization policy, you should become fully aware of the implications of the policy. Determine if you will be protected or equalized on employment-related income only, or on some or all of your income that is not related to your employment. This may be critical if you are earning significant non-employment income.

Giving up Canadian residence

If your departure from Canada constitutes giving up Canadian residence, you will be deemed to have disposed of all of your capital property (except taxable Canadian property; see definition below) at its fair market value at that date, and will be subject to Canadian tax on any capital gains. See page 107 for a discussion of the new rules regarding the elimination of the capital gains exemption.

Tax Tip 22

If you have taxable Canadian property that is a share of a QSBC (qualifying small business corporation) or a qualified farm property and you have not used the enhanced $400,000 capital gains exemption, consider selling such properties with accrued capital gains to your spouse. In this way, you can use your enhanced capital gains exemption. This should be done prior to leaving Canada; if you dispose of the property after you have terminated Canadian residence, any capital gain will be subject to tax in Canada and you will not be able to shelter any of it with the enhanced capital gains exemption.

You will be required to file a part-year Canadian income tax return in the year in which you leave Canada. Ordinarily, you will report your worldwide income up to your date of departure. Additional Canadian tax liabilities could arise if you continue to carry on business or continue to be employed in Canada after you move away.

Canada's rules relating to a principal residence differ from those of other countries. If you intend to sell your home, your professional advisor can help you decide if you should dispose of it before or after you move. If you wish to rent out your home while you are away, you will be deemed to have disposed of it for proceeds equal to its fair market value, both when you convert your home to a rental property and when you reoccupy it as your principal residence. You may defer tax that would otherwise be payable on a capital gain arising as a result of the deemed disposition rules by electing for there to be no change in the use of your principal residence. Whether this election is beneficial to you will depend on how long you will be outside Canada and if you intend to return.

Prior to leaving Canada, you should discuss with your professional tax advisor the tax implications of exercising your Canadian stock options, of receiving payments from your former employer after you have left Canada in respect of services rendered in Canada, of interest earned in your RRSP, etc. The timing of your move will also be critical and will depend on the taxation year of the foreign country as well as on its tax rates compared with those in Canada.

Taking up Canadian residence

If you are taking up residence in Canada, you will generally be deemed to have acquired all of your capital property (except taxable Canadian property, defined below) at its fair market value on the date you take up residence. Any gain or loss on a subsequent disposition of that property will be calculated with reference to this deemed cost.

In the year in which you take up residence, you will be required to file a part-year income tax return. In that return, you report your world income from the date of taking up residence in Canada, plus certain types of income that you received during the part of the year when you were not a Canadian resident. In respect of your non-resident period, you must include: income from business carried on in Canada; income from employment duties performed in Canada; and capital gains realized on the disposition of taxable Canadian property (defined below).

Tax Tip 23

Before taking up Canadian residence, you should ensure that you and your professional tax advisor have discussed the implications of the types of income you may be receiving both prior to and after entering Canada, as well as the timing of the receipt of various types of income. In particular, you should review any foreign incentive compensation that might be payable to you. Depending on the circumstances, you might want to arrange to receive income such as bonuses, stock options and payments from profit sharing plans prior to entering Canada.

If you will be selling your foreign residence and acquiring a Canadian one, it is probably more beneficial for you to sell the former before taking up Canadian residence. If you intend to rent out your foreign home, you will be subject to tax in Canada on the net rental income. If you will also be subject to tax on rental income in your "home" country, you should evaluate the benefits of renting out your home versus leaving it vacant or even disposing of it.

You should also consider the timing of your arrival in Canada. The best date will depend on your tax liabilities in both the country you are leaving and in Canada. Your professional advisor can help you make a detailed estimate.

Taxable Canadian property

Taxable Canadian property includes, among other things, real property (land and buildings, for example), capital property used in carrying on business in Canada, shares of a private corporation that is resident or deemed to be resident in Canada, and shares of a public corporation if at any time during the five years immediately preceding a disposition of those shares, the non-resident and persons with whom he or she did not deal at arm's length owned 25% or more of the issued shares of any class of its capital stock.

Unlike other capital property, you are not deemed to have disposed of taxable Canadian property when you give up your Canadian residence because when you do ultimately dispose of it you are required to file a Canadian income tax return and pay tax on any resulting capital gains.

You may elect to deem other capital property to be taxable Canadian property. If you make this election, you must provide

Revenue Canada with acceptable security equal to the amount of tax that would have been payable on the deemed disposition of the property had you not made the election.

Making this election could improve your cash flow. If the deemed disposition rules apply, you have to pay any tax on a resulting capital gain even though you have not actually disposed of anything and have not received any proceeds. If you make the election (and can post sufficient security) you will not have to come up with the cash immediately.

If you make the election, you should exclude enough capital property to allow you to deduct the unused portion of your capital gains deduction, to the extent that you are in a position to make a late filed capital gains exemption election (see page 107). Keep in mind that any further increase in the value of the property you have elected to be treated as taxable Canadian property will be subject to Canadian tax when you actually dispose of it.

This election has pitfalls, so you should discuss it with your advisor before proceeding.

⚜ Québec

If you are resident in Québec, the comments above generally apply to Québec taxes. However, the following exceptions should be noted:

• Gain Sharing Plan

Amounts received by an employee of certain manufacturing corporations under a qualifying gain sharing plan may be deducted in the calculation of Québec taxable income to a maximum of $3,000 per year. A cumulative maximum of $6,000 applies for the five-year period starting in the year of registration of the first plan in which the employee participates.

The plan must be registered by the Minister of Revenue before January 1, 1996.

Tax treatment of certain clothing allowances

A recent court case indicated that the reimbursement to an employee of distinctive clothing required by the employer will not be taxable. In December, 1994, Québec introduced a measure under which a reasonable allowance given to an employee for the acquisition or upkeep of distinctive clothing will not be included in income, if the employee is required to do so under the employment contract. This change will apply as of the 1995 taxation year.

Québec Sales Tax

• Introduction of a single sales tax rate

The rate applicable to properties, services and immoveables is 6.5%. The rates for insurance premiums are 5% or 9%.

• Purchase of a new home

A rebate equal to 36% of the QST paid on the purchase of a new home costing $175,000 or less is available. A decreasing rebate is also granted on a house costing between $175,000 and $200,000.

• Sales of used road vehicles

The price of used road vehicles on which the QST applies is the higher of the consideration paid by the purchaser and the value of the vehicle given in the Canadian Red Book less $500.

• Property or services acquired in the course of employment

The QST system allows an individual who is an employee of a registrant or a member of a registrant partnership to claim a rebate of the QST paid in regard to properties or services acquired in the course of his or her employment, if the expense relating to the acquisition is deductible in calculating his or her income. The individual could not claim a rebate on the property or service on which the input tax refunds were restricted, such as the purchase or rental of an automobile, fuel, telephone services, electricity and meals and entertainment. As a result of the elimination of the restrictions, all employees and partners of a registered business will be entitled to claim a rebate of the QST paid in regard to the properties and services covered by the restrictions, if the QST is payable after July 31, 1995 and is not paid before August 1, 1995.

Refundable child tax credit

The tax deduction for child care expenses will be replaced by a refundable tax credit equal to a percentage of the amount paid during the year for child care, up to a maximum of $5,000. The rate of tax credit will be based on net family income, as indicated in the table below.

	From	To	Tax credit as a % of eligible expenses
Net family income	$0	$10,000	From 75% to 44%
	$10,000	$34,000	40%
	$34,000	$48,000	From 39% to 27%
	$48,000	∞	26.4%

The amount of expenses eligible for the tax credit for the year is determined by the rules used for the child care expense deduction. The refundable tax credit may be claimed by either spouse.

• Tuition fees

The amount of tuition fees is used as the basis for the determination of the non refundable tax credit. In Québec, tuition fees are deductible only by the student, and cannot be transferred to the student's father or mother. However, a person upon whom the student is dependent may increase his or her dependent child credit if the student is registered full-time in a post-secondary institution. The person requesting the credit must file form Releve 8 with his or her Québec income tax return.

Health services fund contribution

Until recently, only employers paid a health services tax based on employment earnings of their employees. The health services tax has been extended to individuals. The tax is paid by individuals resident in Québec on December 31 as part of their overall income tax bill.

The health services tax is payable on notional "total income", including net business income, investment income, pension or retirement income and taxable capital gains. Excluded from the calculation are those items already subject to the employer health tax (e.g., wages), the gross-up on dividends from Canadian corporations amounts received as Old Age Security benefits and social security benefits.

Certain deductions are permitted in arriving at "total income", including amounts subject to the federal clawback, expenditures incurred to earn investment income, and a general exemption of $5,000.

This contribution is eligible for a non-refundable tax credit of 20% in the individual income tax return.

Temporary assignments in Québec

If you are a non-resident of Canada and you were employed in Québec at any time in the year or in a previous year, you will generally be subject to Québec tax on your employment income and will be required to file a Québec income tax return.

Temporary assignments outside Canada

If you are a Canadian, resided in Québec during 1995, and have been or will be employed abroad for 30 consecutive days or more beginning in the year or the preceding year, you may be allowed a deduction in computing net income equal to all or part of the employment income earned abroad. A full deduction is available if you are abroad for 12 periods of 30 consecutive days or more. This deduction is available for the same types of employers and activities as those mentioned in this chapter for the federal overseas employment tax credit (see page 62). In addition, the following activities are eligible for this deduction:

- the setting up of an automated office system, data processing system or telephone data system or similar system, if that activity is the principal purpose of the contract;

- scientific or technical services; and

- management or administration related to an activity covered by the deduction for workers outside Québec.

Beginning in 1995, the deduction is granted in the determination of taxable (rather than net) income.

Taxable Québec property

Québec has rules similar to those applicable to taxable Canadian property, but they apply only to property situated in Québec that is referred to as "taxable Québec property".

An exception to the general rule is that Québec will remit income tax of an individual non-resident of Canada, not doing business in Canada, realizing a capital gain on sale of shares of a corporation resident in Québec other than a public corporation. The taxpayer will, however, pay the 52% federal non-resident surtax on basic federal tax.

• Tax holiday for employees of an international financial centre (IFC)

A two-year tax holiday may be granted to foreign employees of an
IFC specializing in the field of international financial transactions.
In addition, following this two-year period, under certain conditions, those employees may be eligible for an income tax exemption
on allowances paid to them, up to a maximum of 50% of their basic
eligible salary.

Beginning in 1995, the IFC deduction reduces the taxpayer's
taxable income, rather than net income.

• Extension of the tax holiday granted to foreign researchers

To further encourage researchers specializing in R&D to come to
Québec, the measure granting a two-year tax holiday to foreign
researchers has been renewed, under the same terms as those provided under current tax legislation, for an additional period of three
years. Thus, a two-year tax holiday may be granted to a foreign
researcher whose employment contract is signed prior to January 1,
1997 and whose salary constitutes, for the employer, an R&D
expenditure made in Québec no later than December 31, 1998.

Other Québec exceptions

In Québec, receipts for moving expenses must be filed with the tax
return.

Since 1993, in the case of salaried employees paid on commission,
expenses — which may not be deducted in excess of any commissions paid — must be reduced by an amount not exceeding the lesser
of $750 and 6% of total compensation (salary plus commissions).

An individual, other than a trust, has the choice of excluding
from his or her income, in the year in which he or she receives it, a
retroactive payment of at least $300. Retroactive payments include

72 employment income received as the result of a judgment or an agreement between parties in judicial proceedings or alimony arrears. This choice will enable individuals to pay any tax related to retroactive payment as if they had received the payment in the years to which it applied. This measure is applicable to amounts received after December 31, 1993.

Québec generally follows the terms of the tax treaties signed by Canada regarding what is excluded from income. The only separate tax treaty that Québec has entered into is with France.

Owners/Managers

Owners/Managers

What's new?

- Prescribed interest rate on overdue taxes to be increased by 2 percent (proposed).

- Opportunities for tax deferral on business income to be eliminated (proposed).

Although "owner/manager" is not a term found in the Income Tax Act, it is a convenient way of referring to anybody who owns and runs a business. This chapter deals first with unincorporated businesses, and then with private companies.

Unincorporated businesses

Carrying on business

The distinction between income from a business and income from employment or from investments is important. If you are indeed in business, you will be able to deduct reasonable business expenses not deductible by an employee or an investor.

For tax purposes, a business includes a profession, calling, trade, manufacture, and just about anything else that could possibly be considered a business. Being employed or holding an office, however, is not a business.

If you are self-employed, i.e., you are not an employee and you have not formed a corporation through which you will provide your services, then you must determine whether you are in business. This will not generally pose a problem if you are earning your living from the activity. Generally, you must have a reasonable expectation of profit from the activity for it to be considered a business, and you must pursue the activity in a manner likely to bring you a profit. Although you need not produce a profit immediately, or even have a history of making profits, you must have a reasonable chance of doing so.

An individual can have more than one business, in which case the profits of each must be calculated separately.

If you carry on an unincorporated business, you may be able to make a late filed election to recognize capital gains accrued to February 22, 1994 on capital property (see page 107).

Employed versus self-employed

Whether you are employed or self-employed is not always easy to determine. The answer will depend on your particular circumstances, and often boils down to how much control the person paying for your services exercises over your work. For example, if the payer controls your work hours, requires you to work on his premises and furnishes you with all the equipment, supplies and office help that you need, you likely would still be considered an employee in the eyes of Revenue Canada. If you provide services to a number of different parties and you determine the nature and degree of service and are in a position to prioritize their demands, you are likely self-employed. Other tests include whether you provide your own tools, whether you have an opportunity for profit, and whether you have a risk of loss.

Partnerships

An unincorporated business can be carried on as a proprietorship or a partnership. Each partner is taxed on his or her share of the partnership income in essentially the same way as a proprietor. Based on a predetermined formula, the partnership computes the income that is allocated to each partner. A partner reports the allocated share and deducts expenses incurred personally, such as interest and automobile expenses, to determine his or her net income from the business.

Tax Tip 24

A husband and wife, or other family members, can carry on a business through a partnership. It is generally advisable to have a written partnership agreement to support the profit-sharing formula and the basis of contributions to the business in the event that Revenue Canada raises questions.

Tax Tip 25

Partnerships with more than five partners are required to file annual financial information. The partnership provides reporting slips to partners for inclusion in their own returns.

Professionals

Professionals may carry on business as sole proprietors, partners, or, depending on the legislation and the rules of the professional bodies, through corporations. Designated professionals (accountants, chiropractors, dentists, lawyers, medical doctors and veterinarians) are permitted to elect to exclude the value of work in progress from income. If they do not make the election, they follow the normal accrual rules and report income as it is earned.

Instalments

A self-employed individual earning business or professional income must pay tax directly to Revenue Canada. Quarterly instalments of tax are due as follows:

No deadlines		Deadline on 15th of month
January	February	**March**
April	May	**June**
July	August	**September**
October	November	**December**

- The prescribed rate of interest charged during a calendar quarter on late or deficient payments of tax is set each quarter. The table shows the most recent prescribed rates:

		Prescribed rate*		
		Other than Québec	Québec	
Quarter of 1995	1st	8%	9% or 6.25%**	
	2nd	10%	11% or 6.25%**	
	3rd	13% or 11%**	12% or 6.25%**	
	4th	11% or 9%**	11% or 6.25%**	

* The rate for deemed interest on employee and shareholder loans is lower than the rates shown (see page 23).

** The lower rate applies to amounts owed to taxpayers.

Additional penalties may also be imposed on late or deficient tax instalments if interest in excess of $1,000 is owing.

Choice of year-end

The 1995 federal budget contained a proposal that took everyone by surprise. Up until the budget announcement, an individual could have chosen to have the tax year for his or her business end at any time in the year. A careful selection of a year-end could have resulted in a deferral of tax. This important planning strategy is no longer available.

A bit of background should put the significance of this change into perspective. Although a taxation year for an individual was generally defined to be a calendar year, individual proprietors of a business could have selected taxation periods that ended on any day of the year. Further, individuals who were members of partnerships reported their share of partnership income in the calendar year in which the partnership tax year ended. This rule effectively enabled income to be shifted from one year to another for income tax purposes. Although tax would ultimately have to have been paid when a business ended or was sold, there were still opportunities for significant deferral in the meantime. Indeed, complex business structures evolved over the years that achieved income deferral of 23 months (and possibly more).

Of course, the downside to income deferral was the inherent income tax liability that would ultimately have to be paid on retirement, or on the sale of, or withdrawal from, the business. Without proper planning, a tremendous financial burden could have resulted.

In a continuing effort to control tax deferral, the government has proposed that for fiscal periods that begin after 1994, proprietorships, professional corporations and certain partnerships must report income on a calendar year basis. The proposals contain transitional relief: the additional 1995 income that would otherwise have been taxed in 1995, may be brought into income via a reserve mechanism over 10 years (effectively 5 percent of the additional income the first year, 10 percent for each of the next 8 years and 15 percent for the final year).

A number of recent changes to the original budget proposals are worthy of note:

- Taxpayers who cease a particular business but carry on a "similar" business will continue to be eligible for the transitional relief. For example, a partner in a law firm who leaves to join another law practice after 1995 will continue to be eligible for transitional relief on his or her 1995 income (assuming that the law practice carries on a similar business).

- Eligible taxpayers will be able to retain off-calendar year fiscal ends provided an election adopting an alternative method of calculating income is filed with Revenue Canada. This measure is intended to provide relief for taxpayers with sound, non-tax business reasons for having an off-calendar year-end (for example, because of a natural business cycle or ease of administration). Eligible taxpayers are individuals and partnerships all the members of which are individuals. An eligible taxpayer that elects this method (it appears to be a one-time election as opposed to an annual one), can request a subsequent change in year-end to a calendar year. Once this is done, however, the taxpayer cannot then change back to an off-calendar year-end. Note that this election is effectively for accounting and financial reporting purposes only. For tax purposes, the reported income will have to be adjusted each year to a calendar year-end basis.

- Professional corporations that are not members of a partnership are excluded from the calendar year-end requirement. Professional corporations include corporations that carry on the professional practice of an accountant, dentist, lawyer, medical doctor, veterinarian or chiropractor.

The alternative income method may or may not achieve the most favourable results, i.e., each situation must be evaluated separately.

Tax Tip 26

The proposals dealing with off-calendar year-ends are new and detailed and there are still areas of uncertainty. You should consider meeting with your professional advisor to discuss the general implications of the proposals or the consequences of making the alternative income method election.

To accommodate the accounting and reporting requirements for the calendar year-end proposals, the deadline for filing income tax returns for individuals with business income from a sole proprietorship or partnership has been extended from April 30 to June 15. The change is effective for 1995 income tax returns which are due June 15, 1996.

Tax Tip 27

If you are affected by the new rules requiring that you adopt a calendar year for your business, bear in mind that you must have the same year-end for GST purposes. You're last GST reporting period in 1995 will end on December 31. Subsequent reporting periods will be determined on the basis of the calendar year. If the due date for your income tax return has been extended to June 15, your annual GST return will be due at the same time.

Automobiles

The rules for self-employed individuals are not nearly as complex as those for employees who are supplied with a car by their employers. The restrictions on capital cost allowance claims, monthly interest charges and monthly lease payments that apply to employees claiming automobile expenses, however, apply equally to the self-employed. To make the most of automobile expense claims, you should keep records of expenses incurred as well as details of personal and business kilometres driven.

Tax Tip 28

You do not have to file supporting vouchers or documents with your income tax return but you should keep them in case they are requested by Revenue Canada. They may turn out to be crucial if you are challenged.

If you use a car partly for business and partly for personal purposes, the deductible amount of car expenses is:

$$[\text{operating expenses} + \text{fixed expenses}]$$
$$\times$$
$$\left[\frac{\text{distance driven to earn business income}}{\text{total distance driven}} \right]$$

Expenses incurred in travelling between different premises of the same business are deductible. Expenses incurred in travelling from your home are not deductible, unless you can establish that your home is the base of your business operations. If you have an office or other fixed place of business located elsewhere, your home will not be regarded as the base of your business operations.

The fact that you render all your services at some other persons' place of business will not necessarily make that place your base, and you may still be able to deduct costs of travelling there from your base at home.

If you are a GST registrant, you may be eligible to claim input tax credits for a portion of the GST you paid on reasonable car expenses.

If you are paying automobile allowances to employees, you may deduct those allowances only to the extent that they do not exceed the limits in the table below. If you choose to pay your employees more than the allowable amounts, you cannot deduct the excess unless the full amount of the allowances is taxable in the employees' hands. If this is the case, you should ensure that your employees keep records of the distance they drive and provide you with their records so that you can support your claims. The employees will be able to deduct their business-related expenses and may be better off than they would have been with a nontaxable receipt.

If you are a GST registrant, you may be able to claim a notional input tax credit (7/107 of the allowance paid) to the extent the allowance is both reasonable (i.e., not taxable to the employee) and deductible to you.

		Maximum deductible automobile allowance (per kilometre)	
		All provinces	Both territories
Business driving in the year	First 5,000 kilometres	$0.31	$0.35
	Beyond 5,000 kilometres	$0.25	$0.29

82 Depreciable assets

Although everyday business expenses can be deducted from business income, the cost of capital assets is deductible over a longer period. This is accomplished through the capital cost allowance (CCA) rules, which provide varying rates of write-off, depending on the type of assets involved.

For example, office equipment and furniture are depreciated at a rate of 20% per annum; the rate for general purpose computers and systems software and for automobiles is 30%; and the rate for a building acquired after 1987 is usually 4%. All are calculated on a declining-balance basis.

Generally, in the year in which you buy an asset, CCA is limited to one-half of the rate to which you would ordinarily be entitled. In addition, if your fiscal period is less than a year, you will be required to prorate the CCA amount otherwise determined.

Since CCA is based on the undepreciated capital cost of assets at the end of the year, you will not be able to claim CCA in the year in which you dispose of a business asset unless you continue to own other similar assets that are pooled for CCA purposes with the asset that you sold. On the other hand, you may be entitled to a terminal loss if there is a balance in the class at the end of the year, but no assets.

The CCA rules also permit a taxpayer to elect to place eligible property in a separate class for CCA purposes. Eligible property includes general-purpose electronic data processing equipment, photocopiers and certain electronic communications equipment such as facsimile transmission devices and telephone and related ancillary equipment, if the cost is $1,000 or more.

A separate class election does not change the specified CCA rate on the equipment. Rather, it allows a taxpayer to calculate a separate CCA deduction on one or more particular pieces of equipment. The separate class election ensures that, on the disposition of all the property in the class, any remaining undepreciated cost of the equipment may be fully deductible as a terminal loss. The election benefits taxpayers who acquire eligible equipment that depreciates faster than is implicit in the CCA rate for property of that class. The election must be made in the income tax return for the taxation year in which the property is acquired.

Tax Tip 29

Timing is an important consideration when you are purchasing and selling capital assets. Try to purchase assets before the end of your fiscal year so that you are at least entitled to claim one-half of the normal CCA. When disposing of an asset, try to time the sale after year end so that the full CCA claim is made in the previous year. Generally, you must take delivery of an asset and put it into use in order to claim CCA in the first year.

Office in the home

If you operate an office in your home, you can claim supplies and other expenses that are entirely associated with the business, such as a business phone. Expenses that are shared with the operation of the home, such as utilities, insurance, property taxes, rent and mortgage interest are generally apportioned according to the space used. Depreciation on your home is also deductible, but this will reduce your claim for the principal residence exemption on the sale of your home. Normally, claiming depreciation expense on your home offers little or no advantage.

For your work space to qualify as being used exclusively to earn business income and for regularly and continually meeting your clients, customers or patients, the space set aside for your business must be a room or rooms used exclusively for the business. Setting up a computer and filing cabinets at one end of the living room will not entitle you to claim home office expenses.

If you operate a full-time business out of your home, you will be able to deduct eligible expenses that relate to the work space. If you operate a part-time business, or have other office space out of which you conduct your business, you may be denied a deduction for office in the home expenses.

Tax Tip 30

Home office expenses may be deducted only from income earned from the business carried on in the home, i.e., they may not be deducted from other sources of income. You may, however, carry excess expenses forward to a future year and deduct them from income generated by the business.

Business meals and entertainment expenses

Fifty percent of business meals and entertainment expenses are deductible for tax purposes. A similar restriction applies for purposes of the GST. Accordingly, only 50% of the GST paid on business meals and entertainment expenses may be recovered as an input tax credit.

Tax Tip 31

Meal and entertainment expenses specifically identified on your invoice and billed directly back to your clients are not subject to the 50% limitation.

Retirement plans

If you have an unincorporated business, contributions to an RRSP may be the only avenue available to you to accumulate retirement savings. Your net income from the business, i.e., business income after expenses, is considered to be earned income for the purposes

of determining the maximum amount that you may contribute to
your RRSP. (see page 39 for more details about proposals to reduce
and delay the phase-in of RRSP contribution limits)

If you incorporate your business (see below), you could establish
an IPP (Individual Pension Plan) for yourself (see page 44). As discussed below, the decision to incorporate is complicated, and the
opportunity to establish an IPP is only one factor that should be
considered.

Salaries to spouse and children

If your spouse or children work in the business, salaries paid to
them will be deductible for tax purposes as long as the wages are
reasonable in relation to the work performed. Of course, the wages
received will be taxable in their hands.

Tax Tip 32

Salaries paid to your spouse or children will enable them to
make their own RRSP contributions and to contribute to the
Canada or Québec Pension Plans.

Private companies

Setting up the corporation

Unlike a sole proprietorship or a partnership, a corporation is a separate legal entity, an artificial person required to file a tax return and
pay taxes quite separate from its owners. You may transfer your business assets to a corporation, generally without tax consequences to
you, subject to certain restrictions. In addition to holding shares of
the corporation (equity), you may also hold debt.

Tax Tip 33

You will incur expenses in establishing and maintaining a corporation that you would not have with an unincorporated business. You should evaluate carefully both the timing and consequences of incorporating to see if the benefits outweigh the costs.

Tax deferral

The income from an unincorporated business is included in your personal income tax return and, therefore, taxed at your personal marginal tax rate. In contrast, if you incorporate your business, its income belongs to the corporation, and will be taxed at corporate rates. Your personal income tax return will be affected only to the extent that the corporation distributes its earnings to you as salary, dividends, or interest.

The rate of corporate tax will depend on the type of income the corporation is earning as well as on the province(s) in which it carries on business. For example, up to $200,000 of active business income may be taxed at a combined federal and provincial rate as low as about 18% (even lower if a provincial tax holiday applies). The top marginal rate for an individual earning the same type of income directly would be about triple the corporate rate.

The preferential tax rate for very large private corporations has been eliminated. The $200,000 business limit is reduced on a straight line basis for Canadian-controlled private corporations (CCPCs) with taxable capital employed in Canada of between $10 and $15 million in the preceding year. This eliminates the benefit of the small business deduction for those CCPCs with taxable capital of $15 million or more. This measure applies to taxation years ending after June 30, 1994.

If you incorporate your business and retain earnings in the corporation for growth, you will be able to defer tax to the extent that the earnings are not distributed to you.

Integration

If you are the sole shareholder of a corporation, you and the corporation constitute two separate tax-paying entities. Salary that the corporation pays you is an expense that reduces the income of the corporation. For you, it is income.

The corporation will pay tax on its taxable income; income that is distributed to you from the corporation by way of dividends will be subject to a second tier of tax through the personal tax system. The concept of integration mitigates the effects of this potential double incidence of tax.

According to the integration concept, income earned through a corporation and distributed to an individual shareholder should attract the same amount of tax as if that individual had earned the income directly. In practice, however, integration would work perfectly only if the combined federal and provincial rate of tax is 20% for a corporation and 43.5% for an individual, and if there are no surtaxes.

Because actual corporate and personal tax rates differ from the rates necessary to achieve perfect integration, your total taxes will vary depending on whether income comes directly to you or through a corporation. The differences will depend on the type of income, your province of residence, and the jurisdiction in which the corporation carries on business.

Whether earning income directly or through a corporation is preferable will depend on your personal circumstances. Active business income earned by a corporation, taxed at the small business rate and distributed as a dividend will usually attract less total tax than if you earned the income directly. On the other hand, income taxed at the top corporate rate and subsequently distributed to a shareholder in the top personal tax rate band will suffer double taxation.

Tax Tip 34

Incorporating your business involves making decisions that are both emotional and practical. Complex issues must be addressed, and the choices you make can be costly to undo. Ensure that your professional tax advisor is involved every step of the way.

Refer as well to the discussion regarding investment holding companies on page 131.

Tax Tip 35

Corporations are not subject to Alternative Minimum Tax (AMT) (refer to page 195 for details about AMT works). Accordingly, investments that would trigger an AMT liability for an individual can instead be held by a holding company. A caveat, however: moving certain investments into a holding corporation may not be advantageous if you would lose tax shelter deductions associated with those investments.

Salary versus dividends

One of the major decisions for an owner-managed corporation is the split between salary and dividends. Your personal tax position as owner/manager, as well as that of the corporation itself, must be taken into account in determining the optimum compensation package.

Several rules of thumb help determine the best amount to be paid as salary to owners and the amount to be taxed in the corporation and subsequently distributed as dividends. (Refer to the **Integration** section above, as well as to Tax Tip 36 and discussion below.)

The rules of thumb assume that all amounts paid are reasonable in the circumstances, do not take cash requirements for living expenses into account, and do not consider a possible sale of the business and the capital gains exemption discussed below.

Tax Tip 36

Using salary or bonuses to reduce the active business income of the corporation to $200,000 annually will generally be advantageous to the owner-managed corporation.

Consider paying salary, rather than dividends, whenever the combined federal and provincial tax rate of the corporation exceeds 20%. This will generally hold true when the corporation is earning business income that is not eligible for the small business deduction.

This approach should be reviewed annually to ensure that it is still valid in the circumstances. If payroll taxes are substantial, for example, dividends may be preferable to salary. If the corporation is eligible for a provincial tax holiday, has investment tax credits to use up or has losses carried forward to reduce taxable income, the effective rate may be less than the statutory rate and this strategy may change.

If the corporate rate is 20% or less, paying salary to the owner/manager may be desirable if dividends, when taken with other tax preference items, would subject the owner/manager to AMT.

Tax Tip 37

The salary/dividend mix will affect your tax instalment requirements. Ensure that you and your corporation are remitting the appropriate amounts.

Tax Tip 38

The accrual of a bonus may be preferable to the payment of salary. A bonus paid within 180 days of a corporate year-end will be deductible to the corporation; personal tax will be withheld when the bonus is paid.

Tax Tip 39

Consider paying yourself sufficient salary to enable you to

90

make maximum Canada or Québec Pension Plan contributions, as well as to contribute the maximum to your RRSP. The contribution limit for your RRSP is based on 18% of your earned income in the previous year. The maximum you can contribute to your RRSP in 1995 is $14,500, which means that you must have earned income of $80,556 in 1994 to make the maximum contribution to your RRSP in 1995. (You will need earned income of $75,000 in 1995 to make the maximum RRSP contribution in 1996, which is $13,500.)

See page 38 for details on RRSPs, including new proposals to reduce and delay the phase-in of maximum contribution limits.

Salaries to spouse and children

A corporation may provide an opportunity for income splitting with your spouse or children. Salaries may be paid to family members as long as services are actually performed and the amount of salaries and wages is reasonable. Generally, salaries would be considered to be reasonable if they are representative of an amount that would have to be paid to an arm's length party for similar services.

Paying reasonable wages to family members for actual services rendered has four advantages:

- the salaries will be deductible to the corporation;

- the salaries will be taxed in the hands of the recipients, and depending on the circumstances, probably at rates lower than the top marginal rate;

- the salaries will enable family members to contribute to their own RRSPs; and

- the tuition fee and education tax credits may mean that salaries paid to children attending university may attract little or no tax at all.

Directors' fees

In addition to the role you perform in your own company, you may also be a director, either of another corporation or of your own. If you are a director and are earning directors' fees, those fees are considered to be employment income and must be included on your tax return. Directors' fees are earned income for the purposes of determining how much you can contribute to your or a spousal RRSP. Refer to page 205 as well for a discussion concerning directors' liability.

$500,000 (or $400,000) enhanced capital gains exemption

Tax Tip 40

When you start a business, keep the business assets in a corporation separate from one that holds investment or non-business assets.

Shares of Qualifying Small Business Corporations may be eligible for an enhanced capital gains exemption of $400,000 ($500,000 if you haven't used the $100,000 capital gains exemption. Refer to page 112 for further details.) A small business corporation (SBC) is generally defined as a Canadian-controlled private corporation (CCPC), all or substantially all the assets of which (more than 90% according to Revenue Canada) are used in an active business carried on primarily in Canada. The corporation must be an SBC when the shares are disposed of and the shares must not have been held by anyone other than the taxpayer or related persons throughout the immediately preceding 24 months. In addition, throughout the same period, more than 50% of the fair market value of the assets of the corporation must be used in an active business it carries on primarily in Canada.

Tax Tip 41

Removing any non-qualifying assets from your corporation now will help you meet the "all or substantially all" test in the definition of an SBC when the shares are eventually sold or transferred.

Tax Tip 42

If the shares in your small business corporation have substantial accrued capital gains, consider electing to sell some of the shares to your spouse at fair market value, triggering a capital gain, up to $400,000 of which could be exempt. Professional tax advice is a must because of alternative minimum tax (AMT) and other considerations.

Election for Private Corporations Going Public

Although shares of a public corporation do not qualify as small business corporation shares, individuals may benefit from the enhanced capital gains exemption when a small business corporation is about to go public. An individual may elect to be treated as having disposed of all of the shares of a class of the capital stock of the small business corporation immediately before it becomes a public corporation. The individual will have to specify an amount to be the deemed proceeds of disposition. The proceeds may be the adjusted cost base of the shares or any higher amount up to their fair market value. The individual will be treated as having reacquired the shares immediately after the elected disposition at a cost equal to the specified proceeds. These new provisions will enable an individual to claim the enhanced capital gains exemption in respect of the disposition of the qualifying shares.

Planning around your CNIL

A corporation may provide you with some flexibility in arranging your personal concerns. If you will realize capital gains in the year from the disposition of Qualified Small Business Corporation shares that will not be sheltered from tax by the enhanced capital gains exemption because you have cumulative net investment losses (CNILs), consider arranging to receive sufficient interest or dividend income from the corporation to eliminate your CNIL.

This strategy may fully or partially restore your access to the enhanced capital gains exemption (see page 115 for more about CNILs).

⚜ Québec

If you are an owner/manager residing in Québec, the following differences in the Québec legislation should be noted:

Depreciable assets

Québec has a 100% CCA deduction for:

• computers;

• systems software; and

• machinery and equipment,

used for manufacturing and processing in Québec, without the half-year rule applying.

The same tax treatment is granted for intangible property acquired after May 16, 1989, such as patents, licences, permits (but not trademarks and industrial drawings), knowledge, know-how, techniques, processes or formulae, whether protected or not, acquired in order to implement an innovation or an invention.

94 | Instalments

The Québec prescribed rate of interest charged on late or deficient instalments of tax for the third quarter of 1995 is 12%. Additional interest at the rate of 10% per annum is payable on any late or deficient instalment that is less than 90% of the required instalment.

Health services fund contribution

For more information about this new contribution, please refer to page 69.

Annual information forms and registration

Forms to be filed with Revenue Québec (e.g., partnership forms) differ from their federal counterparts. In addition, to do business in Québec, every partnership, sole proprietorship and legal person must register with the Inspecteur génèral des institutions financières, who can be reached at (418) 643-3625.

New deduction for artists

In the 1995 taxation year, certain artists may claim a maximum deduction of $15,000 in calculating taxable income. This deduction will be reduced by 1.5 times the artist's entire income for the year in excess of $20,000 from copyrights of which he or she is the first holder. Therefore, no deduction may be claimed if the income derived from the distribution of works created by the artist exceeds $30,000 for the year.

Investors

Investors

What's new?

- Opportunities to use general capital gains exemption may still exist.

- Complex rules may deny losses on transfers of property among affiliated persons (proposed).

- The 1995 federal budget changes the incentives for Canadian films (proposed).

- Investment holding companies become less attractive (proposed).

You are an investor even if you do not have an extensive portfolio. If you own your home or maintain a bank account you should review this chapter.

Astute investors never lose sight of the fact that it is the after-tax result of their activities that matters, not the nominal yield on their investments. Tax is only one element in the complex process of making investment decisions. The investment's yield and risk should always be considered ahead of income tax aspects. Although tax itself seldom motivates a particular transaction, it can be a crucial factor when deciding among alternative investments with similar pre-tax yields.

Financial rewards from investment fall into two broad categories for tax purposes: investment income and capital gains. This chapter covers both, along with tax shelters (investments with a significant tax reduction component).

Investment income

Interest and dividends

Interest and dividends are taxed differently. All interest income you received and generally all interest income that accrued to you during the year is fully taxable in your hands. Even a small amount of interest on your savings account for which you did not receive a T5 slip from the bank is taxable.

Dividends from taxable Canadian corporations are included in your income along with a 25% "gross-up" of the amount you received. You can claim a federal dividend tax credit of 16⅔% of the actual dividend (equivalent to 13⅓% of the grossed-up amount) in arriving at your basic federal tax. You may claim the dividend tax credit only in the year the dividend was received.

How the gross up and dividend tax credit reduce taxes at top marginal rates

Without gross-up and dividend tax credit

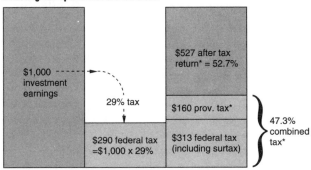

With gross-up and dividend tax credit

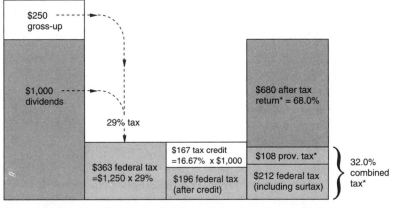

* Provincial tax, and therefore the after-tax return, will vary depending on actual provincial tax rates. This example assumes provincial taxes are 55% of federal taxes (before the federal surtax).

Once the federal surtax is accounted for, the net effect is a reduction in tax of about 15 percentage points, depending on the province or territory.

The bar charts compare the income tax on $1,000 of dividends under the gross-up/credit arrangement and under ordinary rules (i.e., as if no gross-up or credit applied) for a taxpayer at the top rate. The 32.0% combined tax that results from the gross-up and dividend tax credit is about 15 percentage points less than the 47.3% calculated without them.

This approximate 15 percentage point effective reduction in the tax on Canadian dividends means that in 1995, an individual in the top marginal tax bracket would require a gross yield of only about 6% on a dividend to generate the same net after-tax yield as an investment earning 8% interest (see Appendix 3, page 248).

Annual accrual rules

Generally, all interest that accrued in the year on investments you acquired after 1989 must be included in your income for tax purposes, even if you did not actually receive the income. The types of investments to which this rule applies include compound interest debt obligations, deferred annuities and certain life insurance policies. The amount to be reported is the interest earned or accrued during each complete investment year.

For example, if you made a long-term investment on September 1, 1994, the first year's interest must be calculated to the end of August 1995. This amount, whether you receive a T5 slip or not, must be reported on your 1995 income tax return. Similarly, interest accrued on that investment from September 1, 1995 to August 31, 1996 will have to be reported on your 1996 return.

An investment will be treated as having been acquired after 1989 if, after that year, it has been materially altered, for example, by extending its term. Of course, these rules do not apply to interest earned in a statutory deferred income plan such as your RRSP.

Before 1990, you had the choice of reporting accrued interest income from the above-noted securities annually, or deferring tax for up to three years by reporting accrued income every third calendar year after the year of purchase. Accordingly, if you purchased a debt obligation before 1990 (but after November 12, 1981, when the rules changed) and assuming there has been no material change in the terms of the security, you may continue to report accrued interest using the method you have in the past: annually or in the third calendar year after purchase and every three years thereafter.

Tax Tip 43

If you currently hold certain "locked-in" compound interest securities that were acquired before November 13, 1981, you may want to hold on to them. This type of security is not subject to the accrual rules, i.e., you don't have to pay tax on the earnings until the contract matures and you actually receive the interest.

Debt obligations that are held in connection with a U.S. Individual Retirement Account (IRA) are excluded from the accrual rules.

Tax Tip 44

Bonds and other debt instruments that mature should be cashed and reinvested promptly, because they pay no interest after the maturity date. Canada Savings Bonds should be reviewed every October.

Life insurance policies

Life insurance could be an important part of your personal financial planning.

Traditionally, life insurance has often been used as an investment vehicle as well as a means of providing funds to an insured's estate or beneficiaries on the insured's death. Nevertheless, many people opted for "pure" or "term" life insurance policies, which simply paid a stipulated amount on the insured's death, but had no investment component. This preference often reflected the expectation of low investment returns or at least uncertainty about the return available on non-term policies. In recent years, however, the investment aspect has taken on new importance and has become more attractive. One of the major reasons for this is the favourable tax treatment provided for "exempt" policies. Any investment income earned in an exempt policy is exempt from tax. Furthermore, any amounts paid out under an exempt policy on the death of the insured are also exempt from tax. In a sense, the investment element of an exempt policy is a perfect tax shelter, in that the investment income can be earned and paid out without ever having been subject to tax.

To be "exempt", a policy must satisfy certain complex rules covering the relationship between the "pure" insurance portion of the policy and the investment portion.

In effect, these rules require that a certain portion of your premium be used by the insurance company to provide pure insurance coverage, rather than being invested on your behalf. Whether a policy meets these requirements is essentially under the control of the insurance company. Any income accruing on the savings component of a non-exempt policy would be subject to the annual accrual rules referred to in the preceding section.

The other development that has made life insurance more attractive as an investment is that insurance companies have become more willing to disclose mortality and administrative costs, and even to guarantee minimum interest rates. This makes insurance policies easier to understand and makes their investment merits easier to assess.

The tax shelter aspect of an exempt policy has several potential uses, particularly after other tax shelter opportunities (e.g., RRSP contributions) have been exhausted. For example, a life insurance policy could be used:

- to fund supplementary retirement benefits;

- to fund a "retirement compensation arrangement". (This is an arrangement formally provided for under the Income Tax Act for an employer to set aside funds for the retirement of employees. The investment income earned on those funds is normally subject to tax.);

- as a vehicle for making charitable contributions. (A donation tax credit is available for the value of a policy assigned to a charity or for premiums paid on a policy on your life owned by a charity.); or

- in connection with corporate buy-sell arrangements. (If you have a private corporation that owns a policy on your life and pays the premiums, any proceeds received by the corporation increases its capital dividend account (CDA). The balance in a corporation's CDA can be paid out as a tax-free dividend to the corporation's shareholders).

You may also be able to get at the tax-sheltered earnings through taxable draws on the cash surrender value of the policy or by pledging the policy as collateral for a loan.

Another advantage that may be available is protection of your assets. The investment portion of an exempt policy may be excluded by law from the reach of creditors. For more information on this aspect, you should consult your legal advisor.

As with any other tax shelter, an investment in an exempt policy should be assessed on its merits. The insurance business is competitive, so you should shop around before making a decision.

Spouse's Canadian dividends

You may elect to include your spouse's taxable Canadian dividends in your income if by so doing you are able to claim or increase your married status tax credit. All of your spouse's dividends must be transferred. You cannot pick and choose to maximize tax savings.

This strategy works because the tax savings that result from increasing your married status tax credit may more than offset the extra tax that you must pay on the dividends, taking into account the reduced tax on dividends as a result of the dividend tax credit described above.

If adding the dividends to your earnings pushes your net income above the threshold at which the Old Age Security clawback (see page 151) begins to take effect, you may be worse off, and should not make the transfer.

Tax Tip 45

Check to see whether transferring your spouse's Canadian dividends to your tax return will yield significant tax savings. In some cases the saving may amount to several hundred dollars.

Other investment income

Rental properties are a common investment. In some cases, income from an interest in a partnership is reported as investment income.

• Rental income

Net rental income is taxable. To calculate net rental income, current expenses you incur to earn that income are deducted. Most common are interest, heat, electricity, property taxes, water bills, insurance, labour and materials for routine repairs and maintenance, and the cost of advertising for tenants. Condominium management fees are also deductible.

Capital expenditures can be claimed only through the capital cost allowance (CCA) system. Your CCA claim cannot be used to create or increase a loss on the rental property. You should note that while you were once able to claim CCA to increase or create a rental loss on a

Multiple Unit Rental Building (MURB), this special treatment has been discontinued, effective for 1994 and subsequent taxation years.

• Partnership income

If you have an interest in a partnership or limited partnership in which you are not actively engaged, you must report your share of net income or loss on Schedule 5 of your tax return. Normally, you receive a tax reporting package from the general partner that sets out the amount. You should attach this information to your tax return.

If you are a limited partner and a portion of a partnership loss is allocated to you, the investment may be a tax shelter subject to the at-risk rules. (See page 124 for more information about at-risk rules and about recent changes to the provisions dealing with partnership interests.)

You may deduct partnership losses allocated to you only to the extent of your at-risk amount. This means that you cannot deduct losses that exceed the cost of your interest in the partnership, plus profits (or less losses) and other adjustments.

If you have not received a tax reporting package from the general partner, or are uncomfortable with the calculations required, you should talk to your tax advisor.

Deductible interest expense

In general, interest paid or accrued on funds borrowed to earn investment or business income is deductible for tax purposes.

In this context, investment income includes interest and dividends, as well as other sources of income, such as royalties and "passive" rental income. Although investment income in this context does not include capital gains that may be realized on capital property, many investments — such as shares and mutual funds — have the potential of paying dividends or earning income at some future date even if they do not currently. Accordingly, interest expense is generally deductible on funds borrowed to acquire these types of investments.

What happens if you sell the source of your business or property income at a loss? Although the courts have held that interest ceases to be deductible when the source of income to which the interest related no longer exists or is sold and the borrowed money cannot be traced to a replacement income-producing source, new rules provide that interest on borrowed money may continue to be deductible even if the source of the income from business or property is no longer held. The provisions apply when the loss of source of income occurs after 1993.

For example, assume that you borrowed $4,500 in 1993 to acquire shares for your investment portfolio. The shares cost a total of $6,000. The shares decline in value and you sell them for $3,600. You no longer have the shares, but you still owe money to the bank. Under the old rules, the interest on the borrowed funds would no longer be tax-deductible to you.

Under the new rules, and assuming that the shares are sold after 1993, you may be able to continue to deduct all or a portion of your interest expense, depending on what you do with the $3,600 proceeds.

- If you use the $3,600 proceeds to buy another corporation's shares, you will be able to deduct the full amount of your interest on the original borrowing. Here's how it works: since you sold the first shares for 60% of their cost ($6,000 − $3,600), $2,700 (60% of your $4,500 original borrowing) is considered to have been used to acquire the new shares. Since you used the proceeds to buy income-producing property, the interest on the $2,700 is tax-deductible. The new rules will deem the balance of the original borrowing, $1,800, to continue to be used to earn income. Accordingly, you will be able to continue to deduct interest on the $1,800. The result? You may deduct the full amount of interest on the $4,500 that you borrowed.

- Keep the facts the same as above, but this time you use the $3,600 to pay down your credit card balance. What happens to your interest expense? In the same way as in the scenario above, interest on $1,800 continues to be tax-deductible. Interest on the $2,700, however, is no longer deductible because you used that portion of the borrowed funds for personal reasons and not for an income-producing purpose.

The rules will also apply if you borrowed money for the purpose of earning income from a business and the business ceases after 1993. In this situation, you may continue to deduct all or a portion of the interest on money you borrowed for your business depending on how the business is liquidated.

Tax Tip 46

If you must borrow, try to borrow for investment or business purposes before you borrow for personal reasons. Conversely, when repaying debt, always repay loans on which interest is non-deductible before you repay those on which the interest is deductible.

Tax Tip 47

If you are buying Canada Savings Bonds on a payroll savings plan, don't forget to claim a deduction for interest expense. Essentially, you have purchased the bonds at the first of November with borrowed funds and you repay the loan with interest during the year.

Capital gains and losses

Capital gains and losses are realized when you dispose of a property. The word "dispose" is used because you may be subject to special rules that deem you to have disposed of a property under certain circumstances, even if you have not sold the property in the ordinary sense.

For example, a disposition for nil proceeds is deemed to occur when shares have a fair market value of zero, the company is insolvent and has ceased carrying on business, and it is reasonable to expect the corporation to dissolve. No disposition will be deemed to occur if the corporation continues to carry on business within two years of the end of the year.

Property includes real estate, shares in a corporation, an interest in a partnership, depreciable property such as cars or a building, rights or options to purchase or sell property, and even personal property such as antiques, books, or boats.

With the demise of the capital gains exemption (see the next topic), generally three-quarters of your realized capital gains are subject to tax (two-thirds in 1988 and 1989; one-half prior to 1988). Appendix 3 (page 248) compares the tax payable on capital gains to that on other forms of income.

Capital losses are multiplied by the same fractions to determine your allowable capital loss. Allowable capital losses realized in the year must first be used to reduce all taxable capital gains realized in the year. Any balance remaining can then be carried back to the three immediately preceding years to reduce taxable capital gains, and any further balance may be carried forward indefinitely and likewise be used to reduce taxable capital gains.

Realization of significant capital gains may result in liability for alternative minimum tax (AMT). For more details about AMT, see page 193.

Tax Tip 48

Unused losses that have been carried forward from years before 1985 may be applied at a rate of $2,000 per year to reduce income from any other sources.

The $100,000 lifetime capital gains exemption is finally gone after years of speculation. Indeed, the exemption is no longer available for gains realized or accrued after February 22, 1994. If you owned capital property on February 22, 1994 and have not used your entire capital gains exemption, however, all may not be lost. You may make a special election that will allow you to report a capital gain (even though you did not actually sell your property) and claim the capital gains exemption. Although the election should have been filed with your 1994 income tax return, provisions have been made that will allow you to make a late-filed election up to two years after it was normally due, i.e., by April 30, 1997.

An election may be filed with your 1995 or 1996 income tax returns, as long as you prepay a penalty with the late election. The penalty is one-third of 1 percent (.0033) of the deemed taxable capital gain for each month that the election is late.

If you made the special election in your 1994 income tax return, you may revise or rescind the election if you so desire. You have until the end of 1997 to amend an election, again provided a penalty is prepaid. You may not make an amended election if the estimated fair market value in your original election exceeded 110 percent of the actual fair market value.

The penalty is one-third of 1 percent of the deemed taxable capital gain for each month after the month the original election was due. The capital gain deemed realized is reduced by any capital gain recognized in the original election. This means that the penalty is .0033 of the increase, if any, in the taxable capital gain resulting from the amended election over the amount that would have been the taxable capital gain in the original election. Of course, the penalty for an amended election will arise only if the amount designated in the amended election is greater than that made in the original election.

As long as the estimated fair market value in an original election did not exceed 110 percent of the actual fair market value, you may also rescind an election that you filed. A rescinded election must be made by December 31, 1997.

How does the election work? When you file the election, you will be treated as having sold your property on February 22, 1994 and having immediately reacquired it. This will allow you to report capital gains that have accrued on the property up to budget day and to claim the exemption on your 1995 or 1996 income tax return. When the property is sold at a later date, you will add the capital gain that you reported for purposes of the election to the cost of the property. This will reduce any gain in the year of sale and will decrease the tax that you would otherwise have to pay. Any loss will also be based on the elected amount.

For the purposes of the election, you may select the amount that you wish to be the notional proceeds of disposition. The amount that you choose, however, must be greater than the adjusted cost base (ACB) of the property and less than or equal to its fair market value (FMV). Further, the amount must be such that the resulting gain does not exceed the gain that you would otherwise need to recognize to use the capital gains exemption that you have left. For example, if your property has an ACB of $50,000 and a FMV of $200,000 and you have the full $100,000 exemption available to you, you would elect for the deemed proceeds of disposition to be $150,000. This would allow you to shelter the $100,000 capital gain with the $100,000 exemption.

Investors who make an election in respect of depreciable property will not recognize recapture of capital cost allowance (CCA) until the subsequent disposition of the property.

Although the $100,000 capital gains exemption in respect of capital gains realized on the disposition of "non-qualifying property" purchased after February 1992 was eliminated, you may still make the election to use your available capital gains exemption if you own non-qualifying property acquired before that date. Non-qualifying property is generally defined to mean real property that is not used in an active business. Your rental property or your country or vacation home (if they are homes you own in addition to your principal residence) are considered non-qualifying property.

The method of choosing the amount that you will use to make the election on your tax return will be different for non-qualifying property than for other capital property. Because the capital gains exemption in respect of non-qualifying property was eliminated after February 1992, you must use a formula to determine the amount of a gain on the disposition of non-qualifying property that is eligible for the capital gains exemption. Basically, the total gain must be prorated between the periods before March 1992 and after February 1992.

Certain types of properties have special rules to deal with problems arising as a result of the very nature of the properties. For example, provisions dealing with flow-through entities such as mutual fund corporations; mutual fund trusts; investment corporations and mortgage investment corporations; CCPC employee stock option shares; and options are designed to facilitate making the special capital gains exemption election and to ensure that the appropriate results are achieved. Other types of capital property that require specific rules include partially qualified real property, depreciable property, eligible capital property and prospectors' shares. If you own any of these types of properties and are considering making a late-filed election, consider discussing the matter with your professional advisor. Complicated rules may apply and opportunities to make the special capital gains exemption election are limited.

What type of information do you have to compile to make the election? You will need to know the ACB of the property as well as its FMV on February 22, 1994. The ACB of a property usually comprises its original cost (including expenses you paid to buy it such as commissions and legal fees) plus the cost of additions and improvements you made to the property up to February 22, 1994. The FMV of the property is generally the highest dollar value that your property would bring in an open and unrestricted market between a willing buyer and a willing vendor who are acting independently of each other.

Tax Tip 49

If you own a house and a country cottage and have capital gains exemption available, consider making a late-filed election in respect of the property that has increased in value the least. Generally, you will want to preserve the principal residence exemption for the property that has seen the greatest appreciation in value.

Another option to consider if you still have capital gains exemption available: if you own personal-use property that has appreciated in value — jewellery, art, or stamp or coin collections, for example — a late-filed election might allow you to shelter a portion of accrued gains.

Tax Tip 50

Monitor the capital gains and capital losses that you incur after February 22, 1994. Your ability to claim the capital gains exemption with a late-filed election will be eroded if the capital losses that you incur after February 22, 1994 exceed the capital gains that you realize after that date. You may avoid this by delaying the sale of properties with accrued losses until after you have used up any available exemption. Or, sell enough properties with accrued gains to offset your capital losses that would otherwise erode your ability to claim the capital gains exemption.

For publicly traded securities, the FMV will ordinarily be the stock-market-quoted value for February 22, 1994. You can find this information from public listings of transactions on recognized stock exchanges, investment publications, or from your broker. The FMV will be more difficult for securities in privately owned businesses. You may have to obtain a valuation from an accountant or a business valuator. As far as real estate is concerned, the FMV can be determined by professional appraisers. You can also get this information yourself from real estate pamphlets, newspapers, and land registry offices. For items such as art, coins, stamps, and jewellery you will probably have to consult with a dealer or an appraiser.

Tax Tip 51

Ascertain the FMV of your property as soon as possible. The longer you wait, the more difficult it may be to readily determine its value, particularly for property other than publicly traded securities.

What effect will making the election have on you? Making the election will not increase your taxable income, because reporting the gain will be offset by the capital gains exemption. However, it will increase your net income. This may reduce your child tax benefit, GST credit, guaranteed income supplement, provincial tax credits, and some non-refundable tax credits such as the age amount and medical expenses. Making the election may also subject you to minimum tax, increase some provincial taxes, and require you to repay all or part of any social benefits such as OAS.

Tax Tip 52

If you transferred capital property to your spouse and/or children over the last few years in order to use your lifetime capital gains exemption and the property has increased in value, consider whether these family members should make the late-filed election to shelter the accrued gains on their 1995 or 1996 income tax returns.

When the elimination of the $100,000 capital gains exemption was announced, the Finance Minister indicated that the enhanced capital gains exemption for Qualifying Small Business Corporation shares and qualified farm property would be reviewed. At the time of writing, there has been no change to the status of the enhanced exemption. Further, gains on a principal residence also remain exempt.

Tax Tip 53

If you have net capital loss carryovers, or can create a capital loss by selling a particular property, you may be able to shelter the non-exempt portion of a gain realized on the disposition of non-qualifying property.

An additional enhanced $400,000 exemption is available for gains realized on the disposition of shares of a Qualifying Small Business Corporation (QSBC) or on the disposition of a qualified family farm operation.

When the expression "enhanced capital gains exemption" is discussed or referred to in this book, the amount of the exemption will be taken to be $400,000. This assumes that the general lifetime capital gains exemption has already been claimed. For individuals who have not used their $100,000 capital gains exemption in respect of other property, the enhanced exemption will be $500,000.

For the disposition of shares of a corporation to be eligible for the additional $400,000 exemption, the company must be a small business corporation (SBC) at the time of sale. An SBC is generally a Canadian-controlled private corporation (CCPC) that uses all or substantially all of its assets in an active business carried on primarily in Canada by the corporation or a related corporation. Also included are CCPCs whose assets or debt are of "connected" SBCs. "All or substantially all" generally means 90% of fair market value.

The corporation must also comply with restrictive requirements concerning the nature of its assets throughout the relevant holding period (usually two years prior to the date of sale). More than 50% of the fair market value of the assets must be attributable to assets used in active business carried on by it or a related corporation primarily in Canada and/or shares or debt of connected CCPCs that satisfy certain holding period and asset tests. (See page 92 for the exemption when a business goes public.)

If a disposition is deemed to have occurred as a consequence of a shareholder's death and the corporation fails to meet the "all or substantially all" test immediately before the time of death, the opportunity to use the enhanced $400,000 capital gains exemption that otherwise may have been lost could be protected by a measure that is intended to provide relief in such situations. A share that is deemed to have been disposed of on a shareholder's death may constitute a QSBC share at the time of the disposition if it met the "all or substantially all" test at any time within the 12-month period preceding the disposition.

When a corporation holds a life insurance policy under which a shareholder of that corporation is the life insured, an increase in the value of the policy could cause the corporation to fail the asset tests in the definitions described above. This could result in the enhanced gains exemption not being available on the deemed disposition of the shares on the taxpayer's death. For the purposes of the definitions of a QSBC share and a share of the capital stock of a family farm corporation (see below), a relieving provision deems the fair market value of the policy at any time prior to the shareholder's death to be its cash surrender value.

A farm property qualifying for the enhanced $400,000 exemption may be operated as a corporation or a farm partnership. The property must be actively farmed by the taxpayer or family members immediately before the sale to qualify for the exemption, and all or substantially all the assets of the business must be devoted to farming. To qualify, the property may have to meet holding period requirements similar to those for QSBC shares.

The definition of "share of the capital stock of a family farm corporation" clarifies that the property of a family farm corporation is not required to be used in the course of carrying on the business of farming at the time of the disposition of the share. Provided that the other conditions in the definition have been satisfied, prior use of the property throughout any 24-month period ending before the disposition will suffice. A similar clarification exists for an interest in a family farm partnership.

Tax Tip 54

Eligible farm property can be transferred to your children at your cost, so there are no immediate adverse tax consequences, unless an AMT liability arises (see page 193). If you are not going to otherwise use your enhanced $400,000 capital gains exemption, consider electing to transfer the property at a higher value and claiming the exemption. This strategy would "step up" your child's cost base for the farm and he or she will be liable for a much smaller capital gain on any eventual sale.

Reserves

If you sell a capital property at a profit and do not receive the full proceeds at the time of sale or before the end of the calendar year, you may be eligible to claim a reserve. The reserve represents the portion of the gain related to the sale proceeds that are not due until after the end of the year. The reserve is available if you secured the unpaid balance of the purchase price by way of a note payable or a mortgage.

The tax on your gain can be postponed for no longer than five years on most types of capital property. (The reserve limit is extended to ten years for qualified farm property or shares in a small business corporation sold to your children, grandchildren, or great grandchildren.) Each year, beginning with the year of sale, you must bring into income the greater of:

- your capital gain times the proportion of the proceeds actually received prior to the end of the year, less the amount previously recognized; and

- one-fifth (or one-tenth, if appropriate) of the capital gain for each year from the year of sale to the current year.

Amounts brought into income each year under the reserve mechanism are treated as capital gains. The amounts to be included in your income are based on the capital gains inclusion rate in effect in the year the reserve is brought into income.

If you sold a property before November 13, 1981, and proceeds are still outstanding, the five- or ten-year limits on claiming reserves do not apply.

Tax Tip 55

Before the demise of the $100,000 lifetime capital gains exemption, a reserve brought into income after 1987 and that related to a disposition after 1984, was eligible for the exemption. If you had unused exemption available in 1994 and claimed the maximum reserve in respect of uncollected proceeds on a previous disposition, consider requesting an amendment to your 1994 return. Try writing a letter to your Taxation Centre and explain that you wish to claim less than the maximum reserve. This could partially, if not fully, make use of your available capital gains exemption.

Cumulative net investment losses (CNILs)

The CNIL rules were designed to prevent investors from claiming deductions for interest and other investment expenses as well as the capital gains exemption. The elimination of the general lifetime capital gains exemption means that the CNIL will be relevant only in limited circumstances. Net capital gains eligible for the enhanced capital gains exemption on qualifying small business corporation shares or on qualified family farm property, or on capital gains in respect of which a late election will be made must be reduced by your CNIL. If the capital gains exemption is no longer available to you — because you have exhausted your lifetime exemption or the enhanced exemption or because you did not own property on February 22, 1994 on which you can make the special election — you need not be concerned with the CNIL rules at all.

116

Tax Tip 56

If the enhanced capital gains exemption is still available to you and you believe that you might be using it in a particular year, be careful not to get tripped up by a CNIL balance. Your CNIL is calculated to the end of the year. Accordingly, if you plan to claim the enhanced capital gains exemption in 1996 for example, you have until the end of that year to "cure" any CNIL problems.

If you intend to make a late filed election in respect of ordinary gains that accrued to February 22, 1994, check your CNIL balance at the end of 1994 carefully. If you have a CNIL at December 31, 1994, you will have lost the opportunity to make the general capital gains exemption election and will need to consider other strategies.

Your CNIL is computed at the end of a year as the amount by which your investment expenses accumulated after 1987 exceed investment income also accumulated after 1987. Investment income includes the following types of income reported on your tax return:

- interest, the taxable amount of dividends, and other income from investments;

- your share of net income from a partnership in which you are not an active member;

- income from property or from the renting or leasing of rental property; and

- 50% of income relating to the recovery of exploration and development expenses.

Investment expenses generally include the following expenses claimed on your tax return:

- interest and carrying charges relating to investments that yield interest, dividends, and rent;

- interest and carrying charges relating to your interest in a partner-ship in which you are not an active member;

- your share of a loss in a partnership in which you are not an active member;

- 50% of exploration and development expenses claimed; and

- any loss for the year from property or from renting or leasing rental property.

Your interest expense and other eligible investment expenses and losses remain deductible and your access to the enhanced capital gains exemption is merely delayed, not eroded.

For 1992 and subsequent taxation years, your CNIL will be reduced by certain net taxable capital gains in respect of non-qualifying property. This will be achieved by treating the taxable portion of gains on non-qualifying property (i.e., the portion not eligible for the capital gains exemption) as investment income in your CNIL calculation.

Tax Tip 57

If possible, borrow for business purposes as opposed to investment purposes. The interest expense on funds borrowed to carry on a business or profession does not enter into the calculation of your CNIL account.

Special rules for capital gains and losses

• Transfers of losses – proposed new rules

Extensive new rules dealing with losses were proposed in draft legislation announced in April 1995. Although the new provisions primarily affect transfers of losses within corporate groups, individuals may also be affected.

The draft legislation introduces the concept of "affiliated persons". As an individual, you are considered to be affiliated with yourself and with your spouse, but not your children. By virtue of the new affiliated persons concept, you may also find that you are affiliated with a corporation or a partnership. What does this mean to you? Generally, a loss will be denied on transfers of property between affiliated persons. Further, losses will be denied on the redemption of shares of an affiliated company. The new rules generally apply to dispositions of property that occur after April 26, 1995.

This is a complex area. Where transactions dealing with just about anything other than general portfolio investments are concerned, care must be taken to ensure that you do not end up with unintended results. In particular, if you are acquiring or disposing of capital property and corporations, trusts or partnerships in which you have an interest are involved, professional advice is a must.

• Identical properties

When you acquire securities that are exactly the same — Class A common shares of ABC Corp. for example — the shares are pooled for purposes of determining your cost when you sell a portion of your holdings.

Assume, for example, that you buy 200 shares today at $5 each (total cost $1,000) and 100 shares next week at $8 each (total cost $800). Your cost per share for tax purposes is $6 (300 shares for a total cost of $1,800). If you then sell 200 shares at $7 each, your capital gain is $200 ($7 - $6 × 200 shares).

Tax Tip 58

When determining which of your losers to sell prior to year end, ensure that you have indeed accrued losses on the specific securities and that you will not be tripped up by the identical property rules.

• Pre-1972 capital property

Capital gains were not subject to tax before 1972. If you acquired a property before 1972 and you still own it, the portion of any gain accruing to December 31, 1971 is not subject to tax. To determine the portion of the total post-1971 capital gain, you must know the value of the property on V-Day (Valuation Day, basically December 31, 1971) or you may have to have the property valued as of that date, which could be costly. A published list gives V-Day values for publicly traded securities.

If you own identical properties, some of which were acquired before 1972, on a disposition you will be deemed to have sold the pre-1972 properties before those acquired after 1971. Two separate pools will determine the cost of the properties sold; one comprising the properties acquired before 1972, another for those acquired after 1971.

Tax Tip 59

Before having a property evaluated for purposes of determining the non-taxable pre-1972 gain, ensure that the cost of the valuation will be more than offset by the expected tax savings.

• Superficial losses

If during the year you realized capital gains that will be taxable, you may be tempted to dispose of some of your losers to offset the gains. In so doing, however, be careful not to run afoul of the superficial loss rules. A superficial loss arises if you repurchase a security identical to the one you disposed of within 30 days before or after the original sale.

A loss realized on the original sale will be denied if it is a superficial loss. The amount of the loss will simply be added to the cost base of the newly acquired identical property. A similar result occurs if your spouse or a corporation that you control purchases the identical security.

120

• Denial of capital losses

In two specific situations you are not permitted to recognize a loss for tax purposes:

- If you sell capital property to a corporation that is controlled by you or your spouse, the property will be considered to have been transferred to the corporation at your cost, even if you sell the property to the corporation at a loss.

- Losses arising on the sale of capital property to your own or your spouse's RRSP or RRIF will be denied in their entirety. You would be better off selling the property to an arm's length party and making a cash contribution to your RRSP.

• Settlement date

Transactions involving publicly traded securities take place at settlement date: three days after the trading date in the case of Canadian stock exchanges.

Tax Tip 60

Don't undermine your planning strategies by ignoring the settlement date. In 1995, December 20 is probably the last day on which a sale executed through a Canadian stock exchange will be considered a 1995 transaction. Your broker can tell you if foreign exchanges have different settlement dates.

Allowable business investment losses (ABILs)

Losses incurred on the sale of shares or debt in a Small Business Corporation (SBC) are treated differently from ordinary capital losses. An SBC is a Canadian-controlled private corporation (CCPC) that uses all or substantially all of its assets in an active business carried on primarily in Canada (based on a fair market value test). Included are CCPCs whose assets are shares in qualifying SBCs.

An ABIL is calculated in the same manner as an allowable capital loss: three-quarters of the business loss is the ABIL for 1990 and subsequent taxation years.

An ABIL is a reduction in computing net income, unlike an allowable capital loss, which may be used only to reduce taxable capital gains. Any portion of an ABIL not used may be carried back three years and forward seven, the same as normal business losses. After that time, business investment losses become ordinary capital losses.

Bear in mind that:

- Your business investment loss may be reduced by dividends paid after 1971 if you owned the shares before 1972.

- Any ABILs realized will reduce your $400,000 enhanced capital gains exemption. (If you are making a late filed special election, an ABIL will first reduce or eliminate any general capital gains exemption that you claim.)

Tax Tip 61

Although you should consider delaying the realization of an ABIL until you have exhausted your enhanced capital gains exemption, by delaying the recognition of an ABIL, you may be prepaying tax on other income.

Tax Tip 62

The allowable portion of losses realized on the disposition of shares or debt in an SBC may qualify as business investment losses and therefore may be offset against income from all sources. Remember, however, that any post-1984 losses reduce your capital gains exemption.

Principal residence

• What is a principal residence?

The home you occupy is your principal residence. It can be a house, condominium, cottage, mobile home, trailer, or even a live-aboard boat — as long as you occupy it for a portion of the year. A principal residence need not be located in Canada.

Included in the definition of principal residence is the land on which it is situated. Only the amount of land necessary to the enjoyment of the home is included in the definition, usually no more than one-half hectare. (A hectare is 10,000 square metres or about one and one-quarter acres.)

Where zoning bylaws required a larger parcel of land to be included with your house at the time of purchase, more than one-half hectare of land may be included in the principal residence definition.

• Capital gain on disposition

Gains on the sale of a principal residence are generally tax-free. The principal residence exemption is available to a family unit (you and your spouse and your unmarried children under the age of 18) on only one home, in any one particular year or part year, for gains arising since the beginning of 1982. (For gains arising after 1972 and before 1982, each individual is entitled to the principal residence exemption for one house.)

• Change in use

If you start to rent out part or all of your principal residence, an election is available to preserve the principal residence status for up to four consecutive years. You must report the rent received, net of out-of-pocket expenses, as income. If you claim capital cost allowance (depreciation) on the home while it is being rented, Revenue Canada will consider that you have rescinded the election and deem a disposition to have occurred.

In addition, to claim the principal residence designation, you must continue to be a Canadian resident for the period during which you do not occupy the home.

🌐 Foreign residences

Any home that you normally occupy, even on a seasonal basis for only part of the year, may qualify as your principal residence — and this includes a home in another country. You must be a Canadian resident in the years in which you designate your foreign home as your principal residence.

Even though the gain under Canadian rules is tax-free, you may incur a foreign tax liability when you sell your foreign home.

Tax Tip 63

If you estimate that the foreign tax liability will be significant and that you will be entitled to foreign tax credits on your Canadian tax return for foreign taxes paid, you may be better off not claiming the principal residence exemption. Professional advice is essential in this situation.

• Farm property

A farm house is eligible for the principal residence exemption. When you sell the farm, you may prorate the proceeds between the farming property and your principal residence, including no more than one-half hectare of land as part of your principal residence. Alternatively, you may elect to reduce the full amount of the gain on disposition by $1,000 plus another $1,000 for each year of ownership after 1971.

Tax shelters

Tax shelters are investments or business opportunities that offer various types of income tax savings in addition to the potential economic benefits of a successful investment. In most cases, initial tax savings will be complemented by long-term realization of income, if the investment is successful. If the investment does not succeed, the initial tax savings may compensate for part of the economic loss.

The federal government applies specific provisions to restrict or eliminate the benefits of tax-shelter investments, including at-risk rules for limited partnerships, reporting requirements for tax shelter promoters, and capital cost allowance (CCA) restrictions. Other measures may reduce or limit the tax value of tax shelters for some investors. For example, the alternative minimum tax (AMT) limits the benefit of "tax preferences", and cumulative net investment loss (CNIL) rules reduce the amount of the capital gains exemption that may be claimed in a particular year.

Every promoter of a tax shelter is required to obtain an identification number from Revenue Canada. Prior to investing in a new tax shelter, you should confirm that an identification number has been obtained in order to preserve your right to the deductions available to reduce your taxes.

Draft legislation released in April 1995 affects tax shelters in a number of ways. Specifically, the new rules ensure that investors' deductions are limited to funds fully at risk; enhance compliance by ensuring that all tax shelters are appropriately identified; and extend the base of alternative minimum tax to include partnership losses allocated to limited partners and certain passive partners, tax shelter losses and associated carrying charges.

Tax Tip 64

Evaluate the investment potential of a tax shelter in the same way as any other investment. It does not make any economic sense to invest in a shelter if there is little chance of either earning income on your investment or recovering the amount you have at risk, i.e., the amount you invested net of the tax benefits.

Limited partnerships – at-risk rules

Special rules define and limit the extent to which limited partners can use partnership losses and investment tax credits to shelter other income. Losses of a partnership allocated to a limited partner are deductible only to the extent of the partner's at-risk amount at the end of a particular year. A limited partner's at-risk amount at any time is essentially the cost of his or her partnership interest, plus profits or minus drawings and losses, and other adjustments.

Partnership at-risk rules have recently been extended.

The adjusted cost base (ACB) of property that you own reflects your cost of the property and is taken into account in computing a capital gain or loss when you sell the property. In certain circumstances, the ACB of your property may become negative, in which case you would be treated as having realized a capital gain. This rule, however, generally does not apply if the property is a partnership interest. The exception to the rule recognizes that a partner's negative ACB may result from legitimate, and possibly temporary, circumstances, for example, when losses of the partnership are allocated to a partner for tax purposes.

Some tax shelters have been structured to use the exception to the negative ACB rules. To ensure that the at-risk rules cannot be circumvented, limited partners and certain other passive partners are required to report as a capital gain any negative ACB in their partnership interest at the end of a fiscal period of the partnership.

Although the new rules apply to fiscal periods of partnerships ending after February 22, 1994, transitional rules defer the application of the new rules to the fifth fiscal period of the partnership ending after 1994 in the case of film partnerships satisfying certain criteria.

The April 1995 draft legislation proposed numerous changes to the limited partnership rules, including amendments to the "at-risk amount" and an extended definition of "limited partners". Other proposals accommodate changes that arise as a result of the new affiliated persons rules (refer to page 119) and changes required by the elimination of the $100,000 capital gains exemption.

Real estate

Investment in real estate as a tax shelter is not as attractive as it was in the past, because rental losses on real estate cannot be created or

126 increased by claiming capital cost allowance (CCA). In addition, most costs related to the construction period of a project, particularly property taxes and interest expense, must be added to the cost of the land or building and therefore become deductible as depreciation over time, at best, rather than in the first year or two of the investment. Certain soft costs, however, such as rental commissions, guarantees, and landscaping may be deductible in the early years of a project.

Canadian films

Capital cost allowance (CCA) in respect of investments in certified films is limited to a rate of 30% on a declining-balance basis. The rule that normally limits CCA to half the amount that you could otherwise claim in the year of acquisition does not apply. Additional CCA may be claimed up to the lesser of the undepreciated capital cost of certified film productions and the income (net of expenses and the basic 30% CCA) from all certified productions in the year.

The 1995 federal budget proposes to change the existing capital cost allowance tax shelter incentive for Canadian certified productions. For eligible films produced by qualified taxable Canadian corporations, the incentive is to be replaced with a fully refundable tax credit to be known as a "Canadian film credit". The tax credit will equal the lesser of 25 percent of qualified salaries and wages paid after 1994 and 12 percent of the cost of the production. Eligible salaries and wages will be limited to 48 percent of the cost of an eligible production. An eligible production will require a certification as such by the Minister of Canadian Heritage.

Existing CCA incentives will be retained for Canadian certified productions acquired before 1996, the principal photography of which is completed before March 1, 1996. Film productions from 1995 can qualify either for the existing incentives or the Canadian film credit, but not both.

Farming

The attractiveness of a farm shelter from a tax point of view lies primarily in the potential for claiming losses against other sources of income. The key to a farm shelter is the business aspect: to deduct any loss at all, you must have a reasonable expectation of earning a profit from the farming operation. If farming is not at the centre of your livelihood, you may be restricted to $8,750 of losses in a year.

Qualified farm property may be eligible for the enhanced $400,000 capital gains exemption.

Provincial tax shelters

A number of provinces encourage investment in specified areas or industries through various incentive initiatives. Stock savings plans provide tax deductions or credits and venture capital programs are intended to foster investment in small to medium-sized corporations.

Income splitting

Income splitting is having income that normally would be taxed in the hands of the highest income family member taxed at lower rates in the hands of another family member. Tax may even be eliminated if the family member has very little or no income. If you earn income that is taxed at a top marginal rate of say 48% and can arrange to have your spouse earn some of the income so that it is taxed at say 28%, your family will save $20 for every $100 of income earned. Not surprisingly, rules have been established to limit the circumstances in which income splitting may be effective.

Attribution rules

A variety of rules discourage income splitting. Essentially, if you transfer or loan assets to your spouse or a child under 18 years of age, in virtually any manner, the investment income (including interest, dividends, rental income, etc.) will be taxed in your hands, rather than in the hands of your spouse or child. As well, capital gains or losses realized by your spouse on the sale of transferred property will be attributed to you. Attribution of capital gains does not apply on assets transferred to children under 18 years old.

Attribution continues to apply when assets are substituted for the original assets transferred. However, income earned on reinvested income is not attributed to the transferor (see Income on income, page 130).

Although attribution of income ordinarily ceases when a child turns 18, income earned on an investment made by a child age 18 or over (or any other non-arm's length person) using borrowed funds is subject to the attribution rules if one of the main reasons for the loan is to reduce or avoid tax by having the investment income taxed in the child's hands.

The attribution rules may apply not only to loans, but to all situations in which an individual becomes indebted to another non-arm's-length individual. Accordingly, the attribution rules will apply when, for example, the unpaid balance of a purchase price is satisfied by a non-interest-bearing note and one of the main reasons for incurring the indebtedness was to avoid tax by having income included in the hands of the debtor.

In spite of the attribution rules, a number of ways to split income among family members still work. For example, the rules in the Income Tax Act generally do not apply to attribute business income or losses. Income from a partnership is usually income from a business. However, if a taxpayer is a member of a partnership and is a limited partner, an inactive partner or a person who is not engaged in a business similar to that carried on by the partnership except as a member of the partnership, the attribution rules may apply to structures designed to split the partnership income among family members.

Income that results if a loan is made at commercial interest rates and the interest is actually paid within 30 days of year end is also excluded from the attribution rules. Similarly, sales to a spouse at fair market value are not subject to the rules if you receive adequate consideration in return. Because transfers of property between spouses are generally considered to be made at the adjusted cost base of the property, if you want to use this approach, you must elect on your tax return that the transfer take place at fair market value rather than at the adjusted cost base. A contribution to a spousal RRSP is still one of the best income-splitting techniques.

If you are in a higher marginal tax bracket than your spouse, you might consider paying off any balances on your spouse's credit cards. The attribution rules will not apply as long as the credit card debt was not used to acquire income-producing property.

Gifts

If your income is taxed at a higher marginal tax rate than your spouse's, the family will benefit if your spouse earns investment income and you pay family expenses such as credit card balances. Although these payments could be considered gifts to your spouse, no attribution would apply, since the funds are used to pay ordinary costs of running a family and not to generate investment income.

Tax Tip 65
Investment income may be shifted to a child 18 or over by an outright sale or gift of the income-producing property.

Tax Tip 66
Since capital gains on property transferred to children under 18

years of age are not attributed, consider buying capital property with a low yield but high capital gains potential in the names of your children. The income will be attributed to you, but any future capital gains will be taxed in the children's hands, presumably at lower tax rates.

Income on income

Income earned on property that you transfer to your spouse or a child under 18 is generally subject to the income attribution rules and is included in your income for tax purposes. If, however, he or she reinvests the income, income earned on the reinvested income (e.g., interest on interest) is not attributed to you.

Common-law spouse

Two individuals of opposite sex are considered to be spouses of each other when they are cohabiting in a conjugal relationship and they either:

• have so cohabited throughout the preceding 12 months; or

• are the parents of the same child.

Common-law couples are eligible for the married tax credit and may make contributions to spousal RRSPs. Common-law couples are subject to the attribution rules and many other provisions that apply to married couples, including rules that deny losses on the disposition of property to a spouse. Common-law spouses must combine their incomes for the purposes of determining the GST tax credit and the monthly payments under the Child Tax Benefit system (see page 196). The deductibility of child care expenses may be adversely affected. A common-law couple is subject to the same rules that limit a married couple or a family unit to one principal residence.

How does the government monitor common-law couples who choose not to live by the new rules? When does a common-law relationship begin and end? Although marriage, divorce, and separation are legally defined by registration, divorce decrees, separation agreements, etc., whether two people are in a common-law relationship is often unclear. They may even disagree between themselves.

Common-law couples must be careful that they do not fail to anticipate the substantial income tax consequences that may arise as a result of the conduct of their private lives. For example, a legally married individual who leaves his or her spouse, begins living with another person and has a child with that person, may not only have two spouses, but may also inherit an unusually large group of related persons.

Investment holding companies

The tax system contains special rules that are meant to eliminate some of the biases between income earned by an individual and income earned by a corporation. Some of these are designed to ensure that the after-tax return on income realized through a corporation, and subsequently distributed to the shareholder, is roughly the same as if the shareholder had received the income from the investments directly. The system is imperfect, because surtaxes are imposed on individuals in certain provinces and provincial income tax rates vary. In any case, earning interest, dividends, and capital gains in a corporation has usually been advantageous as long as the income is retained in the corporation and the second incidence of tax on distribution is postponed.

Proposals introduced in the two most recent federal budgets in part re-balance the integration system. These tax changes make holding investments through a corporation less attractive. In general terms, the government has proposed to raise taxes payable by corporations on investment income.

132   Every situation is unique and requires a separate analysis. However, there are some general guidelines that you should consider in assessing your strategies.

- If the corporation has a large amount of undistributed income or property with accrued gains, the holding company should be retained (due in large part to the amount of tax that would be payable on a wind-up).

- The largest deferral opportunities remain with dividend-producing assets, rather than interest. No deferral opportunities exist for corporations resident in Alberta, the Yukon and the Northwest Territories, however.

- Larger portfolios generally will be less affected by annual costs of administering a corporation, such as legal and accounting bills, because as a portfolio gets larger, the dollar value of the deferral will increase more rapidly than annual costs.

- Individuals eligible (or about to be) for OAS benefits and whose personal income (excluding investment income) does not exceed $50,000, may still come out further ahead by keeping their investments in a corporation.

- The cost of capital tax must be considered for investment holding companies in Ontario, Québec, British Columbia, Manitoba and Saskatchewan. (The federal Large Corporations Tax must be evaluated for all investment holding companies.)

Tax Tip 67

A regular review of your tax situation, including an annual look at your portfolio, is the best way to determine the most advantageous tax structure in light of any tax rate changes, new legislation and changes to your business.

Rules of thumb for each province and territory

Although the federal budget proposals eliminate the tax advantages associated with holding companies in most Canadian jurisdictions, the effect varies somewhat from province to province.

• Alberta, Yukon, Northwest Territories
Holding companies in provinces and territories with lower rates of personal tax offer no tax advantages.

• Ontario, Newfoundland, British Columbia
In Ontario, Newfoundland and to a lesser extent, British Columbia, there is still opportunity for some deferral of tax, and except for British Columbia, no tax cost overall.

• P.E.I., Nova Scotia, New Brunswick, Québec, Manitoba, Saskatchewan
Deferrals vary in these provinces, which tend to have high overall tax costs. Even with the time value of the deferral, holding investments in a company in these provinces may still give rise to a net tax cost.

Is it still worthwhile to incorporate an investment portfolio?

Many factors should be considered before setting up an investment company. From a purely tax perspective, Ontario, Newfoundland and British Columbia are the only provinces where holding companies still offer some tax deferral and savings, although the savings are small.

Non-tax factors should also be evaluated. Refer to the section below for some of the issues that you should consider.

Should you retain an existing investment holding company?

In light of the federal budget proposals, a shareholder of a holding company has a choice: the holding company can continue to hold existing investments or it can be wound-up. The decision should not be made on tax considerations alone; there may be sound business and other reasons for choosing one route over another. Accordingly, you should discuss your situation with your professional advisor, whether you intend to make changes or live with the status quo. In any event, a variety of factors require your careful consideration, including:

- residency of the individual and the company
- portfolio mix
- continuing costs
- tax consequences of associated corporations
- creditor proofing
- probate fees and estate planning
- cost of winding-up the company

Tax Tip 68

You can use an investment holding company as a discretionary source of dividend income to reduce the balance in your cumulative net investment loss (CNIL) account if and when necessary.

International investors

Canadians investing outside Canada

Canadian residents are taxed on their worldwide incomes. Accordingly, income you earn on investments made in foreign jurisdictions is subject to tax in Canada and must be reported on your income tax return. Whether the funds are deposited into your Canadian bank account or into a bank account in a foreign country is irrelevant.

Generally, you may use the average exchange rate for the year to convert to Canadian dollars both the amount of income to be reported on your tax return and the amount of foreign tax withheld. However, you may use the actual rates at the time the income was received if that is more beneficial. Tax may be withheld in the foreign country from funds remitted to you. You must include the gross amount of earnings, i.e., the amount you received plus the withholding tax. The 25% dividend gross-up rule does not apply, nor is a dividend tax credit available in respect of non-Canadian dividends.

Any foreign tax withheld (up to 15% of the gross foreign investment income) should be used in the foreign tax credit calculation to determine the amount of foreign tax that may be deducted from your Canadian tax liability. Foreign tax withheld in excess of 15% may be deducted in arriving at net income for tax purposes.

Foreign source investment income is subject to the same reporting requirements as Canadian investment income, i.e., interest income accrued but not received must be included in income on an annual basis for investments acquired after 1989 (at least every three years for pre-1990 investments).

Tax Tip 69

A foreign tax credit may be claimed only when amounts are actually paid and foreign taxes withheld. Consequently, no foreign tax credits may be claimed in respect of investment income accrued but not received. Consider filing a waiver with Revenue Canada to keep "open" years in which unpaid interest is reported. This should ensure that the related foreign tax credit will be allowed when amounts are actually received. Be careful to limit the waiver, which is filed on Form T2029, to the accrued investment income reported.

🌏 Non-resident investors in Canada

If you are a non-resident of Canada receiving income from Canadian sources, you may be subject to federal tax in Canada.

If you receive passive investment income such as interest, dividends, royalties, rents and pensions, you are not ordinarily required to file a Canadian income tax return. Instead, the Canadian payor of these types of income is required to pay tax on your behalf by withholding and remitting the appropriate amount of tax at source. The general rate of withholding tax on payments to non-residents is 25%, but the rate may be reduced to between zero and 20%, depending on the type of income and whether a bilateral tax treaty is in force between Canada and the country in which you reside.

If you are a non-resident of Canada and you received certain types of income (for example, alimony payments, pension or superannuation benefits, retiring allowances, RRSP, or RRIF payments) that are otherwise subject to the withholding of tax at source, you may elect to file a Canadian income tax return if the tax reported would be less than the amount withheld. If you do, the election must be made within six months of the end of the calendar year, and you must report all income from Canadian sources. You may generally claim deductions that relate to income reported on the return. In addition, you may be able to claim personal tax credits (see below). Any Canadian tax that has been withheld from income reported on this elective return will be refunded to you if your return shows an overpayment of tax.

Personal tax credits are generally available to an electing non-resident only if more than half of the individual's income is taxable income earned in Canada. In addition, the amount of credits that may be claimed is limited. If you receive rental income from Canada, withholding tax is imposed on the gross amount of rent. You may, however, elect to file a Canadian income tax return and report the rental income and claim related expenses (including capital cost allowance). Again, you would make this election if it reduced your tax liability. You may not claim any other deductions or personal tax credits (i.e., the only income and expenses reported on this type of return must be related to the rental property). However, there is a catch: you will have to file a return for the year in which you dispose of the property and pay tax on any recaptured depreciation or taxable capital gains.

A non-resident of Canada is also subject to Canadian tax on dispositions of taxable Canadian property. Taxable Canadian property includes, among other things, real property (land and buildings, for example), capital property used in carrying on business in Canada, shares of a private corporation that is resident or deemed to be resident in Canada, and shares of a public corporation if at any time during the five years immediately preceding the disposition the non-resident and persons with whom he or she did not deal at arm's length owned 25% or more of the issued shares of any class of its capital stock.

A non-resident will use the same rules to determine taxable capital gains and allowable capital losses as a Canadian resident. Although non-residents are not generally subject to provincial income tax, a federal surtax applies to income earned outside a province. The rate is 52% of basic federal tax.

Tax Tip 70

If you are a non-resident considering investing in Canada, depending on the type of investment and the magnitude of funds to be invested, you may benefit from holding your investment through a corporation, rather than directly. You should discuss your plans with your professional advisor.

Tax Tip 71

If you are a non-resident and plan to become a resident of Canada, consider seeking professional advice regarding opportunities to minimize or defer tax as well as potential liabilities to avoid in the course of relocation.

⚜ **Québec**

If you are an investor resident in Québec, the comments above apply for Québec tax purposes, except for the following:

Measures against the underground economy – buildings

To curb illicit labour in the construction industry, the owners or lessors of rental or commercial buildings must file the T1068 form in which they provide names and other information to be used to identify those who performed work for which an expense is claimed in their income tax return. Certain lessees of commercial buildings should also file the form.

Investment income

You may claim a Québec dividend tax credit of 11.08% of the actual amount of dividends (equivalent to 8.87% of the grossed-up amount) in the calculation of your Québec taxes.

Capital gains or losses

Unused losses that have been carried forward from years before 1985 may be applied at a rate of $1,000 per year to reduce income from any other source.

Cumulative net investment losses (CNILs)

To encourage Québec investments, Québec excludes from the calculation of CNIL deductions for:

- the Québec stock savings plan (QSSP);

- the Cooperative investment plan (CIP);

- Québec business investment companies (QBIC);

- R&D venture capital corporations;

- exploration expenses incurred in Québec; and

- the additional deduction for Québec exploration.

International investors

If the foreign tax credit that may be claimed in calculating your federal tax liability is limited, the balance could be claimed in the calculation of your Québec income taxes. Foreign tax withheld in excess of 15% may be deducted in arriving at net income for tax purposes. Note that for Québec purposes, the strategy of filing a waiver to keep open years in which unpaid interest is reported (see Tax Tip 63 regarding foreign tax credits on page 123) may not be possible. Revenue Québec's position is that only they can initiate waivers to keep years "open."

Non-resident investors in Canada

Special elections allowed under federal tax legislation dealing with:

- certain types of income (for example, alimony payments, pension or superannuation benefits, retiring allowances, RRSP, or RRIF payments); or

- rental income received by a non-resident of Canada,

have no application for Québec tax purposes since no Québec tax is withheld at source.

For Québec tax purposes, any individual who has not resided in Canada at any time during the year but who has:

- been employed in Québec;

- conducted a business in Québec; or

- disposed of a taxable Québec property during the year,

will generally be subject to Québec tax. In such a case, the federal surtax of 52% of basic federal tax that normally applies to income earned outside a province is not applicable.

Québec tax shelters

Québec encourages investment in specified areas or industries through various incentive initiatives. Stock savings plans provide tax deductions and venture capital programs are intended to foster investment in small to medium-sized corporations.

The following are considered to be "Québec tax shelters":

- the Québec stock savings plan (QSSP);

- the Cooperative investment plan (CIP);

- Québec business investment companies (QBIC);

- R&D venture capital corporations; and

- exploration expenses incurred in Québec.

• Québec stock savings plan (QSSP)

A taxpayer who:

- is resident in Québec on the last day of a taxation year; and

- has acquired qualifying shares,

may deduct a portion of the cost of the shares in computing taxable income. The QSSP rule specifies that the last day of the contemplated taxation year is December 31, and not any other taxation year end presumed under special provisions of tax legislation, particularly when a taxpayer ceases to reside in Canada. This rule applies as of the 1994 taxation year.

The settlement data for acquisition of qualifying shares cannot be later than December 31. The deductible portion of the cost of qualifying shares is known as the "adjusted cost" and does not include brokerage, safekeeping, or loan fees related to the shares. The adjusted cost of shares corresponds to a deduction varying between 50% and 100% of the actual cost of the shares, depending on the type of corporation, type of shares and type of investor.

The deduction that may be claimed each year with respect to QSSP shares is limited to 10% of "total income". In this context "total income" means net income minus the capital gains deduction claimed in the year.

QSSP Investment Fund (QIF)

Purchase of QSSP investment fund (QIF) securities allows an individual to take advantage of QSSPs. Generally, to be eligible for a QSSP deduction, the funds collected by the QIF must be invested in QSSP qualified shares, either as part of a public share offering or a private investment made by a qualifying corporation. Rules for QSSP generally apply to investment in a QIF.

• Cooperative investment plan (CIP)

Rules for the deduction for shares of a cooperative investment plan (CIP) are similar to those for shares in a QSSP. Employees of a cooperative who purchase shares in their cooperative under a CIP may benefit from a basic 100% deduction. An additional deduction of 25% is available for investments made after May 2, 1991 under specific programs. Also, an additional 25% will be given for special qualified plans in place after May 16, 1989, raising the deduction levels to 125% or 150%.

Eligible CIP investors also include individuals employed by a partnership in which an eligible cooperative that issues securities eligible for a CIP holds an interest at the time of issue, if the cooperative's share in the revenues or losses of the partnership exceeds 50%.

• Québec business investment companies (QBICs)

Québec business investment companies (QBICs) are special financing vehicles whose activities consist of investing in small and medium-sized private corporations. A QBIC must be registered as such with the Société de développement industriel du Québec (SDI).

A taxpayer who purchases ordinary shares with full voting rights in a QBIC is entitled to a deduction equal to the lesser of:

• 30% of total income; and

• 125% of the amount invested.

The deduction can reach 150% when a QBIC makes an investment in a designated region. Also, if you are an eligible employee of the corporation in which the investment is made, the deduction will be raised to 150% or 175%, depending on whether or not the investment is made in a designated region.

Any amount not claimed in the year may be carried forward to the five subsequent taxation years.

• R&D venture capital corporations

A deduction of 100% of the cost of the share will be granted to shareholders of an R&D venture capital corporation when the scientific research and experimental development expenditure is made by or on behalf of the eligible corporation. The basic deduction is limited to 30% of total income.

Any unused deduction may be carried forward into the five subsequent taxation years.

• Exploration expenses incurred in Québec

To maintain and enhance tax incentives of strategic importance to Québec's economy, the Québec government permits a 25% deduction (reduced from 33⅓% for investments registered before May 15, 1992) with respect to certain exploration expenses incurred in Québec (in addition to the 100% regular deduction). An additional deduction of 50% (increased from 33⅓% for investments registered before May 15, 1992) can be obtained for mining surface exploration expenses.

Retired Persons

Retired Persons

What's new?

- Tax-free rollover of retiring allowances is to be phased out (proposed).

- Payment of OAS benefits modified (proposed).

Retirement is no longer simple to define. Even if you are actively working and earning income, you should read this chapter if you (or your spouse) receive any pension or similar income, or are 64 years old or older. If you are a director of a corporation and are earning directors' fees, those fees are considered to be employment income and must be included on your tax return. Accordingly, you should glance through the chapter dealing with employees to see if anything pertains to you. For example, if you or your spouse are less than 71 years of age, directors' fees are considered to be earned income for the purposes of determining how much you can contribute to your or a spousal RRSP. Refer to page 218 as well for a discussion concerning directors' liability.

Pension income

You must include in income for tax purposes all of the following payments received during the year:

- benefits from your registered retirement savings plans (RRSPs), whether in the form of periodic payments or a lump sum payment;

- amounts received under your registered retirement income funds (RRIFs);

- income from an annuity;

- superannuation or pension benefits;

- Old Age Security (OAS) benefits;

- Canada Pension Plan (CPP) or Québec Pension Plan (QPP) benefits;

- benefits from a deferred profit sharing plan (DPSP);

- foreign pensions;

- retiring allowances; and

- death benefits.

The 1995 federal budget proposes to phase out the provisions permitting an individual to make a tax-free transfer of retiring allowances to an RRSP of up to $2,000 per year of service. Individuals may, however, continue to transfer up to $2,000 per year of service before 1996, plus $1,500 for each year before 1989 in which they earned no pension or DPSP benefits.

A death benefit is generally an amount paid to a spouse or other beneficiary in recognition of the deceased's employment service. If you received a death benefit, you must include the amount received in your income. If the deceased person was your spouse, $10,000 of death benefits are exempt from tax. If you received part of the death benefit in one year and the balance in the next, you may still deduct only $10,000 in total.

You may make tax-free transfers of lump sum amounts from an RPP or DPSP to your RRSP (provided the amounts are transferred directly). However, periodic retirement or pension payments cannot be transferred to an RRSP tax-free.

You may also contribute a lump sum amount received from a U.S. Individual Retirement Account (IRA) to your own RRSP or RPP.

Registered retirement savings plans (RRSPs)

You must arrange to receive a retirement income stream from the funds accumulated in your RRSP by the end of the year in which you turn 71. If you do not, your RRSP will be deregistered in the following year and the entire amount will be included in income and taxed at your normal tax rates.

By converting your RRSP into a program that provides you

with retirement income, the tax shelter benefits of an RRSP are partially retained. Only the amount you actually receive each year is included in your income. Generally, you have two options.

- You can arrange to receive a life or a fixed-term annuity. The fixed-term annuity extends to age 90 and may be based on your age or your spouse's age if he or she is younger than you. Various issuers may offer different features and prices, so allow yourself some time in your 70th year for shopping around, when the time comes to convert to an annuity.

   Both types of annuities may be indexed in a variety of ways so that payments increase each year. Life annuities may be guaranteed for specific periods. Joint annuities based on the lives of both you and your spouse may be arranged. You can also purchase an annuity that may be commuted at your option.

- You can choose to establish a registered retirement income fund (RRIF) with the funds accumulated in your RRSP (see below).

Registered retirement income funds (RRIFs)

A registered retirement income fund (RRIF), as indicated in the RRSP section above, is one of the alternatives you have when converting your mature RRSP to a retirement income stream. As you will see below, you may also establish a RRIF before you turn 71.

   Transfers from an RPP as well as an RRSP may be made to an RRIF of which you are the annuitant. Transfers from an RPP to an RRIF of which your spouse is the annuitant will also qualify if your spouse became the annuitant as a result of marriage breakdown or your death.

   You may have more than one RRIF and you may transfer funds from an RPP or RRSP to your RRIF plans at any time. Since your RRSP must mature (i.e., must be converted to some type of retirement income stream) by the end of the year in which you turn age

71, that is technically the latest time that you can transfer funds from your RRSP to an RRIF. You may also contribute a refund of premiums from a deceased spouse's RRSP to an RRIF tax free.

The RRIF rules allow payments to continue until the death of the annuitant or his or her spouse. Although a specific minimum amount must be paid to you each year, (and taxed in your hands, of course), you may withdraw as much as you want at any time. For example, if you set up an RRIF in the year in which you become 71, you would have to receive payments equal to at least 7.38% of the value in the first year. In the second year you would take 7.48% of the value, and so on.

The minimum percentages that must be withdrawn increase each year until the annuitant (or his or her spouse) reaches the age of 94. For years following, the minimum payment is 20% of the value of the fund at the beginning of each year.

The rules apply to all RRIFs to which funds are transferred after the end of 1992. For most RRIFs that were purchased before the end of 1992 ("qualifying RRIFs"), lower minimum payment percentages apply for ages up to 77. The new minimum payment percentages apply to all RIFFs for ages above 77, regardless of the date of purchase.

RRIFs may also be established before age 71. In that case, the minimum withdrawal amount will continue to be based on your current age to age 90.

Of course, the payments you receive are taxable in your hands. You may have a self-directed RRIF, a mutual fund RRIF, or an RRIF that guarantees to pay a specific interest rate over the life of the plan.

Tax Tip 72

If you have an RRIF from which you receive minimum annual payments based on your age, and you have a spouse who is younger, consider setting up a new RRIF. Minimum payments from the new RRIF can then be based on your spouse's age. The payments will be smaller but will stretch out over more years. (You may not alter the terms of your current RRIF to accommodate the smaller payments.) The minimum payments are just that; you can choose to take out more.

Tax Tip 73

If you are receiving OAS benefits, withdrawals from your RRSP or payments from an RRIF may subject you to the OAS clawback (see pages 151 and 194).

Pension income credit

The pension income tax credit is 17% of pension income or qualified pension income, depending on your age. The federal credit is limited to $170, which translates into $1,000 of pension income. If you are age 65 or over, pension income includes periodic payments from pension plans (including foreign funds or plans), annuities, profit sharing plans, RRSPs, and RRIFs.

If you are under age 65, you may be eligible for the pension income credit if you receive qualified pension income. Qualified pension income includes life annuity payments from a superannuation or pension plan and certain amounts received as a consequence of the death of your spouse (including a common-law spouse): payments from an RRSP, RRIF or DPSP. Lump sum payments do not qualify in any event, nor do CPP or OAS benefits.

The pension income tax credit is transferable to your spouse if you are unable to use all or a portion of it.

Age credit

You are entitled to claim an age credit if you are age 65 or over. The federal age credit is $592 in 1995, which is 17% of the "age amount" of $3,482.

The age credit is subject to an income test. The age amount on which your credit is based will be reduced by 15% of your net income exceeding $25,921 (in 1995). If your income is over $49,134, you will lose the credit entirely. These income thresholds are subject to the same indexing factor as your other personal claim amounts.

The age amount will not be reduced if the credit is transferred from your spouse.

Old Age Security (OAS) clawback

All taxpayers with net income above $53,215 in 1995 must repay all or a portion of Old Age Security benefits received during the year. The repayment is accomplished by means of a special tax calculated as the lesser of OAS benefits received during the year and 15% of your net income (before deducting the clawback) in excess of $53,215.

The OAS clawback rules have three facets:

- you must include the full amount of OAS benefits received in the year in calculating your income for tax purposes;

- the special tax described above is deductible in arriving at your net income; and

- the special tax is added to your federal and provincial tax payable.

The $53,215 threshold is indexed in the same way as personal tax credits and tax brackets.

Effective July, 1996, the 1995 federal budget proposes to implement two new measures that will affect the treatment of OAS payments:

- If your income is above $53,215, your OAS benefit will be reduced before it is sent out to you, rather than being clawed back on your tax return.

- OAS recipients who are no longer resident in Canada will have to file a statement of worldwide income in order to receive their OAS benefits. Non–residents receiving OAS benefits and earning in excess of $53,215 currently enjoy more favourable treatment than Canadian residents because their benefits do not get clawed back.

Tax Tip 74

If you are just over the $53,215 threshold and your spouse's net income is below it, consider splitting your CPP benefits if that will bring your net income below $53,215.

Tax Tip 75

If you are considering making the election to include all of your spouse's taxable Canadian dividends in your income (see page 101), ensure that in so doing you are not subjecting yourself to the OAS clawback.

🌏 Foreign pensions

A foreign pension, including a pension from a U.S. Individual Retirement Account (IRA), must be included in your income and is therefore subject to tax in the same way as a Canadian pension.

Canada has social security agreements with a number of countries. These agreements coordinate benefits from each country and are intended to ensure that an individual is not subject to social security taxes of two countries. If you receive a pension from a country with which Canada has entered into a social security agreement, the taxation of your pension benefits may be affected, and you should either seek professional advice or contact your local Health and Welfare Canada office for further information.

If you receive retirement or survivor's benefits under the U.S. Social Security Act, only one-half of the amount need be included in your income. The first $1,000 that is included in your income is also eligible for the pension income credit (see page 150). Moreover, if you are a Canadian resident receiving U.S. social security benefits and are not a U.S. citizen, the benefits are not subject to U.S. tax. (This exemption does not apply to a U.S. citizen who is a resident of Canada.)

Under the Protocol to the Canada-U.S. Tax Treaty (refer to page 176 for details), starting January 1, 1996 social security benefits will be taxed only in the country that pays them. Residents of Canada who receive U.S. social security payments will pay U.S. tax and will not be subject to Canadian tax on the payments. Similarly, Canadian OAS or CPP payments to a person resident in the U.S. will be subject to Canadian withholding tax and will not be subject to U.S. tax.★

Special expenses

Retirement does not trigger any unusual tax treatment of expenses that some retired people may face. However, the credit for medical expenses may apply more broadly than many people realize. In addition to payments to medical practitioners, payments for prescription drugs and various medical aids, the costs of one full-time attendant at home, full-time care in a nursing home, travelling expenses to obtain medical treatment in your area, and home renovation costs to enable you to get around at home may be deductible.

⚜ Québec

If you are a retired person resident in Québec you should be aware that Québec has fully harmonized its legislation with the federal pension reform. In addition, Québec has entered into social security agreements with a number of countries.

★ The 1996 date assumes that the Protocol is ratified in 1995.

Health services fund

For more information about Health services fund contribution, please refer to page 69.

Special tax credit for retired persons

Québec's income tax system makes various refundable and non-refundable tax credits available to retired or elderly persons. These are more advantageous than their federal counterparts. Chapter 8, **Filing Returns and Paying Your Taxes** (page 203) provides more information.

Property tax assistance for owners over 65

The 1994 Québec budget introduced the possibility, for a municipality, of deferring payment of property taxes payable by an elderly person. If you are a property owner aged 65 or over and are unable to pay your property taxes, contact your municipality, which may be able to help you.

Separated or Divorced Persons

Separated or Divorced Persons

What's new?

* Thibaudeau decision was reversed by the Supreme Court of Canada.

People who are separated or divorced face a special set of tax issues. Those who anticipate separation or divorce must deal with issues that will have tax consequences for many years. These involve the possible distribution of property to satisfy family law requirements, as well as alimony and maintenance payments, income attribution rules, personal tax credits, retirement savings arrangements, and the family's principal residence.

This chapter deals first with issues regarding past marriage break-downs, and then with issues that are important at the time of marriage breakdown.

For income tax purposes, the definition of "spouse" has been extended to a common-law spouse. Two persons of the opposite sex will be considered to be spouses of each other if they are cohabiting in a conjugal relationship and either: (a) have so cohabited throughout the preceding 12 months; or (b) are the parents of the same child. Accordingly, the broad range of provisions in the Income Tax Act that govern the fiscal relations between spouses extends to common-law couples.

The rule means that common-law spouses are entitled to the married status tax credit and are permitted to contribute to spousal RRSPs. It also means that the attribution rules apply, and that common-law spouses must combine their incomes for purposes of the GST credit and the Child Tax Benefit.

The ramifications of the definition may not be entirely clear for some time. The provisions contain terminology that may give rise to some contentious issues. Accordingly, the fact-gathering process for planning may be far more complex and possibly more delicate. Further, there may be some unintended or unpredictable consequences, since the term "spouse" is used in numerous places in the Income Tax Act.

For simplicity, in this chapter "spouse" includes a former spouse.

In the past few years, the tax rules regarding alimony and maintenance payments have been redefined, largely as a result of court cases. The spouse making payments and the spouse receiving payments are both affected. Changes in the family law of several provinces have also contributed to the complexities involved in the division of assets on marriage breakdown.

Tax Tip 76

Counsel provided by a professional tax advisor may be as important on the breakdown of a marriage as legal advice from a divorce lawyer. The repercussions of failing to consider tax issues involved in a divorce or separation agreement can be very costly.

After marriage breakdown

Alimony and maintenance

Alimony or maintenance payments you make to your spouse are deductible for tax purposes if they meet certain criteria. Conversely, if your spouse can deduct payments to you, you must include them in your income. In general, the reverse is also true: if your spouse cannot deduct the payment, you need not include it in your income.

To be deductible, payments must:

- be periodic (lump sum payments do not qualify, even if made by instalment);

- be for the maintenance of the spouse and/or children; and

- generally be made pursuant to a decree, court order, or judgment, or pursuant to a written agreement.

158

In addition, the spouses must be living apart at the time payment is made and throughout the remainder of the year.

The recipient must have complete discretion over how the payments are to be used, except in the case of third-party payments (e.g., mortgage payments made directly to a bank) and payments singled out in the divorce or separation agreement to be devoted to a particular use. Generally, the amount of the payment must be specified, although indexed payments may qualify for a deduction as may certain third-party payments of no specific amount. Indexed payments will qualify only if the formula for adjustment is an acceptable one (for example, payments adjusted in accordance with changes in the Consumer Price Index).

Periodic payments made before the date of a court order or written agreement are generally deductible to the payor if the payments are made in the same year as the order or agreement, or in the preceding year, and if the order or agreement specifically provides that the payments will be included in the income of the spouse and will be deductible by the payor.

Payments made directly to third parties may be deductible if the decree, court order, judgement, or written agreement provides that the payments will be treated as income to the recipient and will be deductible to the payor.

Payments to your estranged spouse for specific purposes, and provided for in more recent decrees, written agreements, etc., may also be deductible, depending on the date of your order or agreement and the purpose of the payment. These must be included in your spouse's income as well.

Tax Tip 77

If you must take legal measures to enforce payment of alimony or maintenance, your legal costs are generally deductible for tax purposes. The legal costs associated with the separation and divorce, however, are not deductible.

You may be able to deduct maintenance payments for your former partner or your children made under a court order on the breakdown of a common-law relationship. Provided that a court order has been issued, the requirements for deductibility by the payor and taxability to the recipient are similar to those discussed for separation or divorce.

Suzanne Thibaudeau v. Her Majesty the Queen

In May 1995, the Supreme Court of Canada ("SCC") reversed the decision of the Federal Court of Appeal ("FCA") in a controversial case dealing with the taxation of child support payments. The FCA had held that a divorced mother with custody of two minor children did not have to include child support payments from her former husband in her income for tax purposes. The court found that the section of the Income Tax Act that requires such amounts to be included in the recipient's income was discriminatory on the basis of family status, i.e., the appellant's status as a separated custodial parent.

The SCC allowed the Minister's appeal and in a 5–2 majority decision, split along gender lines, the SCC found that the Income Tax Act does not infringe the equality rights guaranteed by the Canadian Charter of Rights and Freedoms.

What could this all mean to you? Essentially, nothing has changed regarding the income tax treatment of child support payments. In general, the payer may deduct eligible child support payments, while the recipient must include them in income.

What happens if you filed your 1994 return on the basis of the FCA decision or filed a Notice of Objection for your 1993 (or prior year) return? In the case of the former, any child support payments you received will be included in your income for tax purposes. Additional taxes and interest will likely be assessed. In the latter situation, probably nothing will happen. The Notice of Objection was filed to protect your position in the event that the decision of the FCA was upheld. Since the decision was overturned, your return will stand as you filed it, at least in respect of child support payments.

Although the SCC decision leaves us with the status quo for now, a review of the system dealing with alimony-support tax laws could lead to significant changes.

At the time of marriage breakdown

Income tax is unlikely to be the prime concern of a couple whose marriage is breaking down. Nevertheless, ignoring the tax consequences can be expensive when negotiating future financial arrangements and the division of property.

Lump sum payments or payments of capital are not deductible. Settlements at the time of divorce cannot be deducted by the payor and do not have to be included in the income of the recipient. While the down payment on a home to be occupied by the spouse is not deductible, payments on account of principal and interest on the mortgage are, up to 20% of the original amount of the debt in any one year, provided the payments and tax consequences are specified in the agreement. The spouse benefitting from these payments has to include this amount in income, but may not receive any cash from the payor with which to satisfy any resulting tax liability.

Attribution rules

Income attribution rules cease to apply upon separation or divorce, as long as the spouses are living apart as a result of their marriage breaking down. However, the spouses must jointly elect for capital gains not to be attributed. This election is intended to prevent one spouse from shouldering the unexpected tax liability that could occur if a capital asset were sold for a sizeable gain, most of which accrued during the marriage.

Capital property transferred to a spouse in settlement of rights that arise out of marriage, or to an individual pursuant to a prescribed court order, will be deemed to be transferred at the adjusted cost base of the property, so that no taxable capital gain will result. However, the transferor may elect otherwise in his or her return for the year of the transfer, and therefore govern the taxation of future capital gains. This should be taken into account in negotiating the settlement.

Personal tax credits

If you are paying alimony or maintenance, in the year of marriage breakdown, you may either claim the married status credit to which you normally would be entitled, or deduct your alimony or maintenance payments. You cannot do both. In either case, the spouse receiving the payments must include them in income.

Tax Tip 78

Calculate your tax liability using both methods to determine which works out better in your particular situation. Remember that one method involves a deduction, the other a tax credit.

Child Tax Benefit

Under the Child Tax Benefit system, the mother of eligible children ordinarily receives the non-taxable monthly payments. For the purposes of determining the amount of the payments, family earnings and income are combined. On marriage breakdown, the spouse with whom the child or children will be living may elect within 11 months following the month of breakdown that the former spouse's income be ignored for the purposes of computing the child tax benefit for each subsequent month.

Retirement plans

Tax-free transfers of funds from your RRSP or RRIF to your spouse's or common-law spouse's plan(s) are permitted if the transfer is made pursuant to a decree, court order, or judgement or a written separation agreement and the transfer relates to a division of property.

Retirement income payments eventually made will be taxed in the hands of the spouse who is the annuitant under the plan. As well, attribution rules that discourage one spouse from withdrawing the contributions he or she made to a spousal RRSP do not apply in the case of RRSP transfers or withdrawals on the breakdown of a marriage.

Special tax-free transfers are also allowed in the same circumstances from registered pension plans to other RPPs or RRSPs. Often benefits from a plan are split between the spouses, including common-law spouses. Each spouse would receive the appropriate pension payments directly from the plan and be taxable on amounts received.

Canada Pension Plan (CPP) benefits may also be split between estranged spouses. Each spouse would be taxable on the amount received. To avail yourself of this arrangement, you and your spouse must have been legally married and living together for a minimum of 36 consecutive months.

Principal residence

If you and your spouse own only one home at the time of marriage breakdown, the tax-free status of any accrued gain on the family home will generally be maintained. If one spouse continues to live in the home, he or she will be able to designate the home as a principal residence for each of the years it was occupied during the marriage and after the breakdown. The other spouse could acquire a principal residence after the marriage breakdown, and any gain on its disposition would be sheltered by the principal residence exemption.

The situation is more complex where two homes are owned at the time of marriage breakdown. If each home is sold at some point after a divorce, each spouse will want to claim the principal residence exemption for the years during which they were married.

However, only one home may be designated by a married couple for years after 1981. One spouse would have to forego designating his or her principal residence for the relevant years of marriage. Alternatively, ownership of one of the houses may be transferred at the time of the marriage breakdown and the available principal residence exemptions used at that time (see page 63).

If two houses eligible for principal residence designation are owned at the time of separation or divorce, careful planning will permit maximum use of the principal residence exemption and the greatest deferral of tax.

The elimination of the $100,000 lifetime capital gains exemption in respect of dispositions of real property purchased after February 1992 meant that all or a portion of a capital gain on the disposition of a family property that is not your principal residence would be subject to tax without the benefit of sheltering. Draft legislation will implement the 1994 federal budget proposed to eliminate the $100,000 lifetime capital gains exemption altogether for gains realized or accrued after February 22, 1994. There may however, still be opportunities for you in 1996 to shelter at least a portion of accrued gains on these types of family properties (see page 107).

Québec

If you are a separated or divorced person resident in Québec, please note the following Québec differences:

Legal costs

* In addition to the federal rules regarding the deductibility of legal costs, you may be able to deduct (for Québec tax purposes only),

the legal or extra-legal expenses you paid, as plaintiff or respon-
dent, for a review of the right to receive or the obligation to pay
alimony or a maintenance allowance if certain criteria are met.

However, the legal or extra-legal expenses paid to establish the
initial right to receive or obligation to pay an alimony or maintenance
allowance are not deductible.

Attribution rules

- The Québec income attribution rules are similar to the federal
  rules. The introduction by Québec of Bill 146, an Act to amend
  the Civil Code of Québec, to favour economic equality between
  the spouses, can create some tax complications on death and
  marriage breakdown. Professional advice is recommended.

Exclusion of spouse's income after a separation

- Beginning with the 1994 taxation year, a spouse's income after
  separation will not reduce the married person's tax credit and will
  not have to be added to the total income used to determine tax
  benefits such as the income tax reduction for families, the property
  tax refund, and the refundable tax credit for the QST.

Personal tax credits

In the year of marriage breakdown, Québec generally allows you to
claim the married and dependent credits in addition to the alimony
payments.

Alimony paid in respect of prior years

Effective January 1, 1994, a recipient of alimony paid in respect of prior years may elect to pay the tax owing on the payments as if the alimony were received in the years to which the payments relate, rather than in the year of receipt. If an election is made, the payor must also claim the deduction in the years to which the payments relate.

A non-tax issue

Bill 60 (1995, chapter 18) assented on May 16, 1995 now dictates how the Québec government will enforce judgments awarding periodic support payments. In general, debtors of support will be required to make their support payments to the Minister of Revenue for the benefit of the person receiving support, except when in certain cases, the court decides otherwise. Support payments will be collected either by a deduction at source from amounts paid regularly to the person required to pay support or by a payment order from the Minister, in which case the person paying support will be required to furnish security. Twice a month, the Minister will remit the amount of support that has been collected to the person receiving support. In certain cases, the Minister may pay to the creditor sums to stand in lieu of the support payments.

These new measures take effect December 1, 1995.

Taxpayers with U.S. Connections

Taxpayers with U.S. Connections

What's new?

- Protocol to the Canada–U.S. tax treaty. It is expected to come into force in November 1995.

If you are a Canadian resident working, investing, living, or doing business in the U.S., if you own property in the U.S. or if you have or expect to have coverage under U.S. social security, then you may have a U.S. connection for tax purposes. If you are a U.S. citizen with comparable ties to Canada you should review this chapter as well.

Special issues regarding employees on temporary assignment in or from another country are dealt with elsewhere in this book (see page 58).

The long-awaited and much discussed Protocol that amends the Canada–U.S. Tax Treaty was signed on March 17, 1995. Many of the points discussed in this chapter will be affected by the Protocol. Until the Protocol is ratified by both Canada and the U.S., however, the dates on which most of its provisions come effective remain uncertain. (Refer to page 176 for a discussion of how the Protocol will affect the topics dealt with in this chapter.)

Canada–U.S. Tax Treaty★

The long-awaited and much discussed Protocol that amends the Canada–U.S. Tax Treaty was expected to be ratified in November 1995 as *Personal Tax Strategy* went to print. Many of the points discussed in this chapter will be affected by the Protocol. Once the Protocol has been ratified by both Canada and the U.S. and the effective dates for various provisions are known (see page 176), taxpayers and their advisors will be in a better position to assess its effect.

★ Affected by the Protocol, expected to be ratified November 1995. See page 168.

Rules for the taxation of income earned in one jurisdiction by a resident or citizen of another are complex and depend on the nature, and in some cases the magnitude, of income received from U.S. sources, among other things. As a Canadian resident, non-U.S. citizen, you would not ordinarily be required to file a U.S. income tax return if you are receiving interest from deposits in a U.S. bank or if you are receiving dividends from some U.S. shares (such income may, however, be subject to withholding tax at source). On the other hand, if you are providing services in the U.S. in the capacity of an employee, or if you own property in the U.S., you may have to file a U.S. income tax return, even though you may ultimately not have any tax to pay.

Various provisions in the Canada–U.S. Tax Treaty may be significant to you. The table below shows a few types of payments you might be receiving from the U.S. Bear in mind that individual states

U.S. Withholding rates on payments to individuals★

			Percent of payment or proceeds withheld in the U.S. (in general)
Received from the U.S.	Interest		15%
	Dividends		
	Pension payments	Periodic	
		Lump sum	30%
	Capital gain realized by Canadian resident on disposition of U.S. real property*		10%
	Alimony and maintenance		Exempt
	Employment income earned in the U.S.	Within treaty exemption limits**	
		Non-exempt	Applicable federal and state rates

* May apply for withholding certificate. Gain is also subject to tax at applicable federal (and possibly state) rates.

** Exempt by treaty if:
- remuneration is less than U.S. $10,000;
  or
- the individual was present in the U.S. for less than 184 days and remuneration was not borne by an employer who is a resident of, or has a permanent establishment in, the U.S.

★ Affected by the Protocol, expected to be ratified November 1995. See page 168.

may not recognize treaty benefits, particularly on employment and pension income.

Tax Tip 79

Under U.S. domestic law, interest earned on deposits with U.S. banks is generally free of tax when paid to a non-resident. If withholding tax is deducted at source, you should advise the bank immediately. You may have to provide a Certificate of Foreign Status.

Canadian income tax rules are complex enough on their own, without having to take into account the tax rules of another jurisdiction. You should discuss any transborder issues with your professional tax advisor.

Canadian "Snowbirds"★

Many Canadian "Snowbirds" are required to file a special statement with the U.S. tax authorities.

A Canadian citizen and resident will also be considered to be a U.S. resident for tax purposes by the Internal Revenue Service (IRS) if he or she meets a "substantial presence" test. The individual is deemed to meet this test if he or she is present in the U.S. for 31 days during the year and, if pursuant to the following formula, he or she is present in the U.S. for 183 days or more: $\frac{1}{6}$ of the days in the U.S. in the second previous year plus $\frac{1}{3}$ of the days in the U.S. in the previous year plus all of the days in the current year. Canadians who spend just over four months per year in the U.S. will generally meet this test.

If an individual is considered to be a resident according to the

---

★ Affected by the Protocol, expected to be ratified November 1995. See page 168.

test above, but spends fewer than 183 days in the U.S. in the current year, has a tax home in a foreign country and a "closer connection" with the foreign country, the individual will not be considered to be a U.S. resident and will not have to file a U.S. resident tax return as long as he or she files a statement with the IRS.

A tax home is generally considered to be the country where the individual reports for work or where the individual has his or her regular place of abode. Certain factors are considered in determining whether a "closer connection" exists. These include the location of the individual's permanent home, family, social, and economic ties. The IRS will also consider the location in which the individual holds a driver's licence, voting registration, and country of residence designated on forms and documents.

To claim the "closer connection" exemption, an individual must file Form 8840 or a prescribed statement under penalties of perjury. The statement must contain the following information:

- the individual's name, address, U.S. identification number, and visa number, if any;

- the individual's Canadian passport number;

- the year for which the statement is to apply;

- the number of days of presence in the U.S. during the past three years;

- whether the individual has taken steps to obtain permanent resident status;

- the facts that would indicate a "closer connection" to a foreign country; and

- sufficient evidence to show that the individual has filed a return as a Canadian resident.

The "closer connection" statement must generally be filed by June 15 with the IRS in Philadelphia, Pennsylvania. If a U.S. tax return is otherwise required, the statement should be filed with the return.

172

Failure to file the statement could result in the individual's being treated as a U.S. resident subject to U.S. tax.

Apart from the Canada–U.S. tax treaty, a Canadian resident who does not meet the "closer connection" test, (i.e., who has a U.S. "green card" (permanent residence status) or who spends 183 or more days in the U.S. in a year) will be considered to be a U.S. resident for tax purposes and required to file a U.S. tax return. However, such an individual would probably be considered a resident of Canada under the treaty. As a resident of Canada, the individual will generally be able to exclude non-U.S. income from the U.S. return. The individual will, however, be required to file a treaty-based disclosure form (see below) and disclose his or her world income.

In view of the serious implications, you should consult your professional tax advisor if you regularly spend time in the U.S. or if you have a vacation or retirement home there.

Disclosure of treaty-based filing positions★

Canadian individuals who benefit from the Canada–U.S. tax treaty may have to file a statement disclosing the fact that a treaty provision has been used to reduce or eliminate U.S. tax that would otherwise be payable. In cases in which no U.S. tax return is filed, a disclosure statement may still have to be filed if a taxpayer relies on a treaty-based benefit.

The reporting requirement is waived when the return-based position pertains to, among other things:

- treaty-reduced withholding payments such as interest, dividends, rents, or royalties paid to unrelated parties; and

- a reduction or modification of taxation of income derived from wages and salaries, pensions, annuities, and social security payments.

★ Affected by the Protocol, expected to be ratified November 1995. See page 168.

However, other situations will require disclosure. For example, if a Canadian resident does not meet the "closer connection" test (see "Canadian Snowbirds" above) and is relying on the Canada–U.S. treaty to exclude non-U.S. income from a U.S. return, disclosure will generally be required. When a Canadian relies on a provision of the Canada–U.S. treaty that reduces or modifies the taxation of a gain or loss from the disposition of U.S. real property interests, or claims application of the non-discrimination clause of the treaty, disclosure will also generally be required.

Although it is not an official form, IRS Form 8833 may be used to provide the necessary information. The form, or other similar disclosure statement, should be filed with an individual's tax return. Fairly detailed information must be reported, including the taxpayer's name and address, the nature and amount of the gross receipts on which the treaty benefit is claimed, and a statement of facts relied upon to support each separate position taken.

Penalties for failure to disclose a treaty-based position are stiff. For an individual, the fine is $1,000 per position not disclosed.

Canada–U.S. Social Security Agreement⋆

The reciprocal Social Security Agreement between Canada and the United States coordinates the social security programs that provide old age, disability, survivor, and death benefits of the two countries. It protects the social security rights that Canadian and U.S. migrant workers have earned through a combination of residence status and social insurance contributions. It also provides for continuity of coverage and ensures that a worker will not be contributing to both countries' social security schemes for the same work.

If you receive retirement or survivor benefits under the U.S. Social Security Act, only one-half of the amount need be included

⋆ Affected by the Protocol, expected to be ratified November 1995. See page 168.

174

in your income for Canadian income tax purposes. The first $1,000 is also eligible for the pension income tax credit. Moreover, as long as you are not a U.S. citizen, the benefits are not subject to U.S. tax.

U.S. estate tax★

U.S. federal estate tax rates for non-residents ranging from 18 to 55% may create significant estate tax liabilities for Canadians who die owning U.S. "situs property" having a net realizable value in excess of U.S. $60,000. U.S. situs property includes: real estate (a vacation condominium, a private house, or U.S. real estate used or held in connection with a U.S. business venture); shares of a U.S. corporation (whether public or private); debt obligations issued by U.S. residents (including debt obligations issued by the U.S. government); and other personal property situated in the U.S. (including furnishings, cars, boats, jewellery, and even the value of a membership in a U.S. club).

The U.S. estate tax is levied on the fair market value of property owned by the deceased as of the date of death. Non-recourse debt attributable to U.S. assets, as well as a portion of other liabilities, may be deducted to arrive at the net taxable value of an estate.

Canada has no estate tax. Instead, Canadian income tax law deems a disposition of the decedent's property on death and income tax is levied on the accrued capital gains. Canadian income tax on accrued gains on property that passes from the decedent to the surviving spouse or to a spousal trust can be deferred until the death of the surviving spouse. The opportunity for a Canadian to defer U.S. estate tax until the death of a surviving spouse is more limited. In fact, property bequeathed by an individual to a surviving spouse may be subject to U.S. estate tax twice — once on the death of the individual and again on the death of the spouse.

Canadians who die owning property subject to U.S. estate tax may

---

★ Affected by the Protocol, expected to be ratified November 1995. See page 168.

also be faced with Canadian capital gains tax as a result of the deemed disposition on death rules. There is no relief by way of foreign tax credit for U.S. estate tax payable and no tax treaty protection to eliminate double taxation. Discussions between the Department of Finance of Canada and the Treasury Department of the United States with respect to income and estate tax matters that began in 1990 are continuing. Apparently, the discussions are focusing primarily on the effect of the U.S. federal estate tax and the effects on nationals of both countries of the Canada–U.S. Income Tax Convention. (See also the comments below on the new Tax Protocol.)

Deposits with U.S. banks or savings and loan associations, as well as proceeds from life insurance policies, are excluded from the U.S. taxable estate of a non-resident, non-citizen decedent.

Tax Tip 80

Consider the following suggestions for reducing your U.S. taxable estate:

- Split property with your spouse and/or among your children. Every individual is entitled to his or her own estate tax credit.

- Refinance (non-recourse loans secured by U.S. situs property reduce the net taxable value of an estate).

- Rent rather than buy personal use property, such as cars, boats, and vacation properties.

- Change your investment portfolio and reinvest in Canada or elsewhere.

- Consider the use of a Canadian corporation to hold your U.S. property.

- Evaluate the cost of life insurance as a means of funding a possible U.S. tax liability.

Professional tax advice is a must before you attempt to implement any strategy to reduce or eliminate your exposure to U.S. estate tax.

The Tax Protocol's effect on individuals

Effective Dates

The Protocol will come into effect when it is ratified by both
Canada and the U.S., which is likely to be before 1996. Provisions
affecting U.S. federal estate taxes will be retroactive to November 10,
1988. Withholding tax rates will generally become effective at the
beginning of the second month after the date of ratification. Other
provisions will become effective on the January 1 after ratification
(i.e., January 1, 1996).

Withholding Tax Rates

The withholding tax rate on cross-border interest payments will
drop from 15% to 10%. On dividends, for most individuals the rate
will stay at 15%. Royalties and rents remain subject to a 10% withholding tax rate, except for certain payments in respect of the use of
technology, which become exempt from withholding tax.

Relief from U.S. Federal Estate Taxes

The Protocol provides a possible exemption for a smaller estate and
some tax credit relief for a larger estate. However, Canadians with
real property interests in the U.S. or significant U.S. investments
should still review their portfolio arrangements with a view to taking
advantage of U.S. estate tax planning techniques.

The Protocol establishes a new threshold value for estates in
respect of deaths after November 10, 1988. If the value of the worldwide gross estate of a Canadian resident does not exceed US$1.2
million, the estate will be subject to federal U.S. estate taxes only in
respect of property whose sale would yield a gain that would be taxable to an individual as a result of the provisions in the Treaty that
deal with gains. This property would include real property, resource

property and business property of a permanent establishment.

In addition, a Canadian resident will generally be treated no less favourably than a U.S. citizen with respect to U.S. estate taxes. A Canadian will be entitled to two credits against the estate tax: a marital property credit (of up to US$192,800) for spousal bequests of U.S.-situated property and the so-called "unified credit" (also up to US$192,800).

Any U.S. estate taxes that are paid will be recognized for credit against Canadian income taxes imposed on U.S. source income arising in the year of death.

Amending previously filed U.S. estate tax returns and Canadian income tax returns for the year of death could yield significant tax savings, because the new rules will apply retroactively. Claims for refunds must be filed by the later of one year after the date on which the Protocol enters into force and the end of the statutory period otherwise prescribed by domestic law.

Social Security Payments

Canadian-resident beneficiaries of U.S. retirement arrangements and U.S.-resident beneficiaries of Canadian retirement arrangements will be allowed to elect to defer Canadian or U.S. taxation, respectively, until funds are received from the plans.

Social security benefits will be taxed only in the country that pays them. Residents of Canada who receive U.S. social security payments will pay U.S. tax and will not be subject to Canadian tax on the payments. Similarly, Canadian OAS or CPP benefits paid to a person resident in the U.S. will be subject to Canadian withholding tax and will not be subject to U.S. tax.

Gambling

The Protocol permits Canadian residents who gamble in the U.S. to offset gains with losses resulting from wagering transactions, for the purpose of computing their U.S. tax liability.

⚜ Québec

If you are a Québec resident with a U.S. connection for tax purposes, or if you are a U.S. citizen with comparable ties with Québec, the federal rules generally apply with the following difference.

Québec–U.S. Social Security Agreement

Since Québec has its own social security program, which provides pension, disability, survivor, and death benefits through the Québec Pension Plan, it has entered into its own U.S. Social Security Agreement. The agreement is similar to the one entered into by Canada. If you receive retirement or survivor benefits under the U.S. Social Security Act, only one-half of the amount need be included in your income for Québec income tax purposes. The first $1,000 is also eligible for the pension income tax credit.

Application of the federal Canada–U.S. Tax Protocol

The new Protocol modifying the Canada–U.S. Tax Convention will change the federal tax treatment of receipts of U.S. Social Security. Québec can be expected to follow the federal changes in that regard.

Calculating Your Taxes

Calculating Your Taxes

What's new?

- Measures will affect payment of OAS benefits (proposed).

- Donations of ecologically sensitive land are to be exempted from the 20 percent net income limitation (proposed).

Ultimately your tax has to be calculated — first by you or your advisor, then by Revenue Canada. Even after all the elements in your tax return are determined, calculating your tax can be a confusing exercise, even when you are using the tax tables provided in the Revenue Canada Guide, or a commercial computer program.

This chapter, along with information that Revenue Canada provides, will help guide you through the many steps involved in calculating your tax. Throughout the chapter you will encounter references to the personal tax flowchart (developed especially for this book to show how the various elements in a tax calculation are related). The flowchart appears twice (pages 183 and 193). The second version has an extra section that deals with alternative minimum tax (AMT) that includes boxes referred to by letter (e.g., flowchart box D). All the other boxes are numbered (e.g. flowchart box 4) and are the same in both versions. The chapter, however, will still make sense even if you prefer to ignore the flowcharts.

The appendices (especially Appendix 2 on page 244) can help you estimate the amount of tax you will be required to pay.

As in other chapters, material at the end highlights important additional information and differences for Québec taxpayers.

Taxable income

Total income

Your total income includes income from employment, investments,

taxable capital gains, pensions and business income [flowchart box 1].
These have been discussed in other chapters of this book.

After working out your total income, you calculate your taxable income in two stages: your total income less certain deductions and adjustments equals net income; and net income less other deductions gives you your taxable income.

Deductions

The first set of deductions includes RRSP and RPP contributions, union or professional dues, child care expenses, ABILs, moving expenses, alimony or maintenance payments, and interest and carrying charges for investments [flowchart box 2]. Another important deduction in arriving at net income is the social benefits repayment ("clawback") discussed later in this chapter [flowchart box 14].

Subtracting these deductions from your total income yields your net income [flowchart box 3]. Net income is used in a number of preliminary calculations, such as the "equivalent-to-married" credit.

A second set of deductions [flowchart box 4] includes the capital gains deduction (if applicable), the employee home relocation deduction, stock option and share deductions, and deductions for net capital and non-capital losses from previous years.

Subtracting this second set of deductions from net income produces your taxable income [flowchart box 5].

Taxable income and net income are used in some provinces' surtax calculations (see Appendix 5, page 256).

Federal tax

Federal tax is calculated using your taxable income and the federal marginal rates [flowchart boxes 5 and 6] found in Appendix 4 (page 252) or in schedule 1 of your 1995 tax return. Once you have determined your federal tax, you will have to subtract some tax credits and add the federal surtax. As well, you will have to make a number of other adjustments and calculate provincial (or territorial) income tax before arriving at your actual tax liability for the year.

If your return is straightforward and your taxable income is $59,180 or less, you may be able to use Tax Tables A and B (provided in the government's General Income Tax Guide and Return package) to compute non-refundable tax credits, federal income tax, individual surtax, and provincial tax.

Non-refundable personal, dividend, and other tax credits

Unless you used Table A in the government's tax package, from the amount you have calculated, you deduct your personal and other non-refundable tax credits [flowchart box 8] (including self-employed CPP contributions [flowchart box 13]). These credits are based on amounts you claim. Every taxpayer claims the basic personal amount; other claims depend on individual circumstances: Are you married? Are you age 65 or over? Did you have substantial medical expenses? Did you make any charitable donations?

Your credit is calculated as 17% of the total of these claims (except that higher charitable donations are credited at 29%).

Sufficient credits could reduce your basic federal tax [flowchart box 9] to zero, eliminating your federal and provincial income tax liabilities. They cannot produce a negative amount that would create a refund, unlike some other credits (which are refundable) discussed later.

Appendix 6 (page 262) sets out the various personal tax credits.

• Personal tax credits

Personal tax credits [flowchart box 8] are the first non-refundable tax credits. They reduce your federal tax. Personal tax credits are equal to 17% of your "claim amounts". For example, as noted above, everyone is entitled to claim the basic personal amount, which is $6,456 for 1995. At 17%, the claim translates into a credit of $1,098.

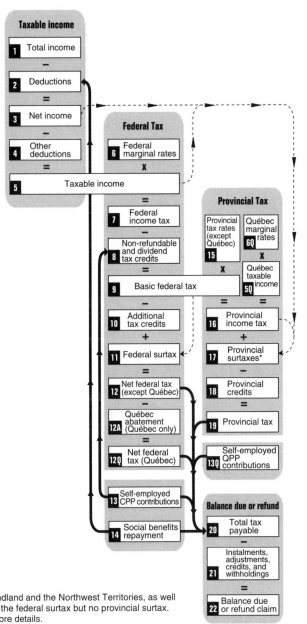

* Residents of Newfoundland and the Northwest Territories, as well
  as non-residents, pay the federal surtax but no provincial surtax.
  See Appendix 5 for more details.

If you are married, you may claim an amount in respect of a spouse you are supporting. The claim, and hence the credit, will be reduced dollar for dollar if your spouse's net income is over $538, dropping to zero at a net income of $5,918.

You may claim an equivalent-to-married credit if you are single, widowed, separated, or divorced and you wholly support a person related to you by blood, marriage, or adoption. Except in the case of a dependent child, the person you are supporting must reside with you in Canada. The person you support must be under 18 years of age, unless that person is your parent or grandparent, or unless the person was dependent on you because of a mental or physical infirmity. The amount of the equivalent-to-married credit is the same as the married credit. Further, only one equivalent-to-married credit may be claimed per household.

Although you may claim only one equivalent-to-married credit, you may also claim credits for dependents (you or your spouse's children, grandchildren, parents, grandparents, brothers, sisters, aunts, uncles, nieces and nephews, and in-laws, too) who are totally dependent on you for support. The dependents must be 18 years of age or older and must be physically or mentally handicapped. The claim amount is $1,583 if the dependent's net income is less than $2,690, dropping to nil at a net income of $4,273.

If you are severely disabled, a disability tax credit is available. Generally, your daily living activities must be markedly restricted and the impairment must have lasted or be expected to last for a continuous period of at least 12 months. A doctor must certify the disability on a prescribed form, the Disability Tax Credit Certificate, which must be filed with your return when you first make your claim. The disability tax credit for 1995 is $720.

A taxpayer may also claim the unused part of a dependent's disability credit. You may claim the credit for a person in respect of whom you claimed the equivalent-to-married credit, or for a dependent child or grandchild who is 18 years of age or over and who has a mental or physical handicap.

Certain non-refundable credits that your spouse does not require to reduce tax payments to zero may be transferred to you. The age, disability, tuition and education fees, and pension income credits are all transferable.

• UI, CPP or QPP credits

If you paid unemployment insurance (UI) premiums or contributed to the CPP or QPP, you are entitled to credits based on your contributions and the maximum required.

• Pension income credit

If you receive various types of pension income, you are entitled to a pension income credit of 17% of eligible pension income, to a maximum credit of $170 (or $1,000 of pension income). The credit is transferable to your spouse to the extent that you are unable to use it (see page 150 for the types of pension income that are eligible for the credit and strategies to ensure that you will be entitled to use it).

• Age credit

You are entitled to claim an age credit if you are age 65 or over. The federal age credit is $592 in 1995, which is 17% of the "age amount" of $3,482.

The age credit is subject to an income test. The age amount on which your credit is based will be reduced by 15% of your net income exceeding $25,921 (in 1995). If your income is over $49,134, you will lose the credit entirely. These income thresholds are subject to the same indexing factor as your other personal claim amounts.

The age amount will not be reduced if the credit is transferred from your spouse.

• Tuition and education tax credits

The federal tuition credit is 17% of eligible tuition fees to the extent that the fees exceed $100. The education credit is 17% of $80, for each month or part of a month that the student was enrolled in a qualifying educational program as a full-time student at a designated educational institution. The student need only be enrolled in a qualifying program; he or she need not be actually attending the designated educational institution. This ensures that the credit is available to students participating in long-distance education programs or correspondence courses. Entitlement to both credits must be supported by Form T2202 or Form T2202A, which the educational institution will provide. Enrollment in either a Canadian or foreign educational institution may entitle the student to a credit.

Tax Tip 81

The tax credits may be transferable from the student to a supporting person, generally a parent, grandparent, or spouse. Only the amount that the student is unable to use to reduce his or her federal tax to zero can be transferred. The total of tuition and education credits that can be transferred is limited to $680.

Tuition fees may be claimed only on a calendar year basis. On your 1995 return, for example, you may only claim fees paid for courses taken between January 1 and December 31, 1995.

• Medical expense tax credit

You may claim a tax credit for medical expenses paid within any 12-month period ending in the year. Expenses for which you are reimbursed, either by your employer or a private or government-sponsored health care plan, are not eligible for the credit. However, few plans reimburse 100% of expenses, and the difference between the amount you actually pay and the amount received from the health plan is a medical expense.

The list of eligible medical expenses is extensive and includes fees paid to a private health or dental plan. Although most of us are pretty good about keeping our receipts for doctor, dentist, and pharmacy bills, we tend to forget about receipts for premiums paid to private plans. Make sure that you and your spouse (and other family members, if appropriate) keep them. The receipts must be attached to your tax returns to be eligible for the credit.

Total eligible medical expenses must first be reduced by the lesser of 3% of your net income and $1,614 in 1995. This amount is indexed annually in the same way as personal tax credits. The $1,614 cap takes effect if your net income is over $53,800. The tax credit is 17% of the amount remaining.

Tax Tip 82

Carefully select the 12-month period for medical expenses. Keep your receipts for 1996 if some 1995 expenses are not claimed on your 1995 return.

Up to $5,000 of part-time attendant care expenses that are not otherwise deductible in computing income qualify for the medical expense tax credit. Eligible expenses are those incurred by or on behalf of a disabled person who qualifies for the disability tax credit in respect of an attendant who is not related to the disabled person.

Also eligible for the medical expense tax credit is the cost of:

- specially trained service animals that assist individuals with severe and prolonged impairment that restricts the use of their arms and legs;

- modifications to the home to enable a person with a severe and permanent mobility restriction to gain access to the home or rooms in it; and

- incontinence products required by reason of a physical impairment.

The list of eligible medical expenses for the purposes of the medical expense tax credit also includes the cost of visual or vibratory signalling devices to those with a hearing impairment and expenses for rehabilitative therapy to adjust for speech or hearing loss, including training in lip reading and sign language.

Charitable donation tax credit

Donations made to registered Canadian charities are eligible for a tax credit on your income tax return. Although the amount of donations that may be claimed in any one year is limited to 20% of your net income, donations in excess of the limit may be carried forward for five years. Donations to specified foreign universities are also eligible for the credit. Donations to other U.S. charities or foreign charities in countries with which Canada has a tax treaty are also eligible, but generally only to the extent that you have income from the foreign jurisdiction. The 20% limitation also applies in the case of foreign donations. More generous rules deal with qualifying donations to the Crown or donations of certified Canadian cultural property.

The 1995 federal budget proposes to eliminate the 20 percent limitation for donations of ecologically sensitive land made after February 27, 1995. Donations must be made to Canadian municipalities and registered charities designated by the Minister of the Environment. Land that is donated must be certified by the Minister to be important to the preservation of Canada's environmental heritage.

You must file official tax receipts with your tax return. (Cancelled cheques are not acceptable.) Otherwise, the tax credit may be disallowed.

The tax credit for charitable donations is two-tiered. The credit is 17% of the first $200 of charitable donations plus 29% on any excess. Either spouse may claim the donations of the other, no matter whose name is on the official receipt.

Tax Tip 83

If you and your spouse donate over $200 in any one year, the tax credit will be larger if one spouse claims the entire amount.

For example, if you and your spouse each donate $200 and claim a tax credit on your own returns for the donations made, your tax credit would be $34 each ($200 x 17%), for a family total of $68. On the other hand, if one of you included the entire amount of donations on your return, the tax credit would be $92 (200 x 17% + $200 x 29%).

Tax advantages are just an added benefit of charitable giving; as with your investment decisions, tax is only one factor. A donation that offers little or no tax benefit should not be rejected on that ground alone.

Tax Tip 84

Watch the timing of your donations. If you donate $400 this year, $200 of your tax credit will be calculated at 17% and $200 at 29%. If, instead, you donate $200 in December and another $200 in January of the following year, your tax credit will be determined using 17% in both years, and your tax credit will be $24 less.

• Dividend tax credit

In addition to deducting non-refundable tax credits from federal tax on taxable income, you are also entitled to a dividend tax credit if you reported dividends from taxable Canadian corporations [flowchart box 8]. On your tax return, the actual amount of your dividend is grossed up by 25%. The dividend tax credit is 13⅓% of this grossed-up or taxable amount of dividends that you reported (see also page 96).

At this point, the amount of basic federal tax [flowchart box 9] is preserved for computing provincial income taxes and the federal surtax, and for comparison with AMT. However, further adjustments enter into the calculation of federal income tax.

The remaining steps in your tax calculation are the same whether you have to pay AMT or not. The only differences are that if you have to pay AMT:

- the basic federal tax [flowchart box 9] is replaced by the "minimum amount" from the AMT calculation; and

- the additional tax credits [flowchart box 10] are replaced by a special foreign tax credit.

Additional tax credits

🌏 Foreign tax credit

You may reduce tax payable by claiming a non-refundable tax credit for income or profits taxes paid to a foreign government [flowchart box 10]. The credit is equal to the lesser of the foreign tax paid and Canadian tax payable on that income. A separate calculation must be made for each foreign country. A separate calculation is also required for business income taxes and non-business income taxes paid to each foreign country. Unusable foreign business income tax credits may be carried back three years and forward seven.

Non-business income taxes do not enjoy the same treatment; however, to the extent that foreign tax on your investment income exceeds 15% of the foreign income, the excess is deductible in computing income subject to tax.

You may also be able to claim a provincial foreign tax credit to the extent that you were unable to claim the entire foreign tax credit on your federal return.

• Political contribution tax credit

You may claim a tax credit on your federal income tax return for contributions made to federal political parties [flowchart box 10]. Official receipts must be filed with your return. Most provinces have similar credits for political contributions to provincial parties.

The credit is calculated as follows: 75% of the first $100; 50% on the next $450 and 33⅓% of any contributions over $550. The maximum credit allowed in any one year is $500, which means that you get no credit for political contributions in excess of $1,150.

Tax Tip 85

Consider spreading your political contributions out over two years. For example, if you contribute $700 in 1995, your federal tax credit will be $350. If instead you contribute $350 in 1995 and $350 in the following year, your tax credits will be $200 each year, a $50 increase.

Federal surtax

The federal individual surtax [flowchart box 11] has two levels, both based on basic federal tax.

The first level applies to everyone: it is 3% of basic federal tax.

The second, the "high-earner" surtax, is determined as 5% of any basic federal tax over $12,500. A taxpayer resident in Canada with the fewest and smallest possible credits and no deductions will begin paying the second-tier surtax after earning approximately $62,195. At that level the federal marginal rate is 29%, so at 8% of basic federal tax the federal surtax adds 2.32% to the marginal rate. For more on the calculation of the federal surtax, see Appendix 4, page 252.

The total federal surtax is added to the federal component of your income tax.

Provincial, territorial, and non-resident taxes

Provincial, territorial, and non-resident taxes provide a tier of income tax that adds roughly 45% to 69% of federal tax [flowchart boxes 9 and 15 to 19] to your tax bill, before any provincial surtaxes are added. Except for Québec, provincial taxes are determined by applying the appropriate provincial rate to basic federal tax (see Appendix 5, page 256). In addition, most provinces have their own systems of surtaxes and tax reductions (see Appendix 5). Outside Québec you do not file a separate provincial tax return; rather, you calculate the provincial tax owing and remit it, along with your federal income tax return and federal balance payable to Ottawa, where it is allocated to the appropriate province.

Québec's tax system is more complex. Rather than calculating tax as a percentage of the federal level, Québec has a parallel system that closely resembles the federal one, but requires a separate return and payments directly to the provincial government [flowchart boxes 5Q to 16]. Refer to the various Québec sections for further details about that province's tax regime.

If you are filing a Québec income tax return, your federal return will also be affected. In recognition of the fact that Québec collects its own taxes, a refundable Québec abatement, simply a credit of 16.5% based on your basic federal tax [flowchart box 12A], is deductible in calculating your net federal tax [flowchart box 12Q].

The Yukon and Northwest Territories also impose taxes comparable to provinces other than Québec.

A Canadian resident individual typically pays provincial tax to the province or territory of which he or she is a resident on December 31. Non-residents of Canada who receive income from Canadian sources (for example, rental income, pensions, annuities, alimony, and capital gains) may be subject to federal tax. Although non-residents will not ordinarily be subject to provincial income tax because they are not resident in a province or territory, they may be subject to a federal surtax that applies to income earned outside a province. This surtax has the effect of putting a non-resident in a position comparable to that faced by a resident. Of course, non-residents earning Canadian source employment or business income may have to pay provincial or territorial tax on such income.

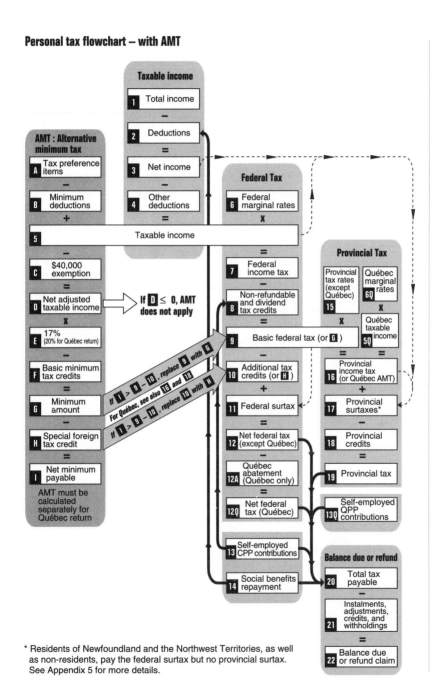

* Residents of Newfoundland and the Northwest Territories, as well as non-residents, pay the federal surtax but no provincial surtax. See Appendix 5 for more details.

194 | ## Social benefit repayment ("clawback")

If you received unemployment insurance (UI) or OAS benefits, you may have to repay a portion, depending on your income. If your net income exceeded $60,840, you must repay a portion of the UI benefits you received [flowchart box 14]. That payment is deductible [flowchart box 2]. The calculation for OAS is outlined elsewhere in this book (along with a discussion of proposed changes to the rules governing payment of OAS benefits)(see page 151).

Balance due or refund claimed

To calculate your total tax payable [flowchart box 20], add:

• the net federal tax [flowchart box 12];

• any self-employed CPP contributions you are required to make [flowchart box 13];

• the "clawback" [flowchart box 14]; and

• total provincial tax [flowchart box 19].

Only a few more items [flowchart box 21] need to be considered before the tax calculation is complete.

You subtract any tax you have already paid, particularly amounts that have been withheld at source, any instalments of tax that you have made throughout the year, and overpayments of CPP or UI premiums. The refundable tax credits, including the investment tax credit and any provincial tax credits are also subtracted [flowchart box 21].

At last you know how much you owe Revenue Canada, or how much Revenue Canada owes you as a refund [flowchart box 22].

Alternative minimum tax (AMT)

If your calculation of taxable income [flowchart box 5] reflects "tax preference items" [flowchart box A★] that lower your tax bill, you should calculate your net adjusted taxable income [flowchart box D★] and your minimum amount [flowchart box G★] to determine if you are liable for alternative minimum tax (AMT).

Tax preference items to be included in adjusted taxable income for this calculation include certain deductions, and income that is subject to special rules. The most common tax preference items are:

- contributions to RPPs, RRSPs, DPSPs (less lump-sum receipts);

- CCA claimed on MURBs and certified film properties (less income before CCA);

- resource expenditures, depletion and resource allowances (less resource income); and

- the non-taxable portion of capital gains.

A non-arm's length sale to realize capital gains may result in a minimum tax liability.

Your minimum amount [flowchart box G★] is calculated by applying a federal rate of 17% [flowchart box E★] to net adjusted taxable income [flowchart box D★]. If your net adjusted taxable income is zero or less, you need not go any further: AMT does not apply to you. While no refundable credits or dividend tax credits are available (although the dividend gross-up is excluded from income), you may deduct basic minimum tax credits [flowchart box F★] to arrive at your minimum amount [flowchart box G★].

You should not have to pay AMT unless your tax preference items exceed the $40,000 exemption [flowchart box C★]. Even then the 17% rate may be lower than your "regular" tax rate, which means you won't be subject to AMT.

★ Refer to Personal Tax flowchart with AMT, page 193.

From your minimum amount, you may deduct a special foreign tax credit [flowchart box H★], leaving you with your net minimum payable [flowchart box I★]. The special foreign tax credit is similar to the regular foreign tax credit, discussed above.

Your net minimum payable [flowchart box I★] is compared to your basic federal tax less additional tax credits [flowchart box 9 less box 10] and the larger amount is used in subsequent tax calculations. Accordingly, if you are liable for AMT, your federal surtax and provincial tax will increase.

AMT is a complex calculation, and there are other more unusual elements to consider. Revenue Canada has provided Form T691 for calculating AMT. You are even better off if you use one of the available computer programs for preparing your return; the calculation will be done automatically.

If you are required to pay AMT, you are entitled to a credit in future years when your basic federal tax [flowchart box 9] exceeds your AMT minimum amount [flowchart box G★] for that year. The credit is the excess of AMT over your regular liability. The carryforward period is seven years, and the credit each year cannot reduce your liability below your AMT amount for that year.

Child Tax Benefit system

The Child Tax Benefit system replaced the system of family allowances, non-refundable child tax credits for children under age 18 and the refundable child tax credit. This system provides the same level of benefit per child to families in similar financial circumstances.

What are the particulars? The Child Tax Benefit is paid monthly, generally to the mother. The benefit is calculated by the government on the basis of tax information from the previous year. The basic benefit of $1,020 per child may be supplemented by:

★ Refer to Personal Tax flowchart with AMT, page 193.

- $75 for the third and each subsequent child in a family; and

- $213 per child under age seven when no child care expenses are claimed.

Low-income working families with children also receive an earned-income supplement of up to $500 per family. The supplement is reduced when family adjusted income exceeds $20,921.

The Child Tax Benefit does not have to be included in your income nor is it recovered on your tax return. The amount of the benefit is, however, reduced by a factor based on net family income and the number of children in the family. In particular, the benefit is reduced by 2.5% of family income in excess of $25,921 for families with one child and 5% of the same amount for families with more than one child.

⚜ Québec

Québec residents do not calculate their provincial taxes as a percentage of federal tax (see Appendix 5, page 256). Instead, Québec has a parallel tax regime that closely resembles the federal system and requires a separate provincial return in addition to the one you file for federal purposes. The calculation of Québec taxable income is slightly different [flowchart box 5Q] (page 183 or 193) as are the marginal rates that are applied to Québec taxable income [flowchart box 6Q] to determine your Québec tax liability.

If you pay your federal tax by instalments, you may have to remit instalments of tax to Québec as well (see page 208).

Credits and deductions

Although most of the federal tax credits [flowchart box 8] are available in Québec, the amounts and types of credits differ somewhat.

198 | ## Changes in the determination of net income

- Tuition fees are considered to be deductions in the determination of net income in Québec, whereas they are a non-refundable tax credit for federal tax purposes.

- Child care expenses have become refundable tax credits in Québec, although they remain a deduction in determining income for federal tax purposes.

Non-refundable tax credits

• Amount for a person living alone

A credit of $1,050 may be claimed in Québec by a person living alone and who:

- during all of 1995, maintained a self-contained domestic establishment in which no other person lived during the year, with the exception of a person for whom an amount for dependent children (i.e., under 18 or a full-time student) could be claimed;

- was not married at any time in 1995 or, if married, was not supporting his or her spouse; and

- did not have a common-law spouse at any time in 1995 or, if he or she did, was not supporting the common-law spouse.

The fact that a person made alimony payments entitling him or her to a deduction does not in itself mean that the person is considered to have been supporting a spouse or common-law spouse.

This amount may not be claimed in the income tax return of a deceased person.

• Married person tax credit

A spouse's income after separation does not reduce the married person's tax credit and does not have to be added to the total income used to determine tax benefits such as the income tax reduction for families, the property tax refund and the refundable tax credit for the QST.

• Tax credit for dependent children
The amount of the tax credit for a second and each subsequent child is $2,400 for 1995.

• Tax credit for the elderly
Taxpayers aged 65 or over are entitled, for Québec income tax purposes, to a non-refundable tax credit equal to 20% of $2,200, representing a reduction of up to $440 in the amount of income tax they have to pay. Under the federal tax system, taxpayers aged 65 or over are also entitled to a non-refundable tax credit. However, since the federal budget of February 22, 1994, this federal old age tax credit is subject to an income test as of 1995. The Québec tax system is not harmonized with this federal measure.

• Tax credit for political contributions
The Québec tax credit for contributions to a political party is increased from $140 to $250 for 1995.

Refundable tax credits

• Tax credit for elderly persons housed by others
Québec grants a refundable tax credit to persons who lodge the elderly. The amount on which this tax credit is based is $2,750, which corresponds to a credit of $550 for each adult lodged in 1995. To be eligible for this tax credit, the housed parent must be aged 70 or over, or 60 or over and suffering from a prolonged, severe mental or physical disability.

• Tax credit for employees of the elderly

Although a proposal in the 1994 Québec budget would have introduced a tax credit for persons aged 65 or over who incur costs by hiring persons to do domestic work, this measure appears to have been dropped.

• Tax credit for adoption expenses

The 1995 refundable tax credit for adoption expenses is equal to 20% of eligible adoption expenses incurred for a child and paid by the individual or by his or her spouse. It may not exceed $2,000 per child (up from $1,000 in 1994), for a maximum of $10,000 in eligible expenses (up from $5,000 in 1994). This measure applies to final adoption orders handed down after December 31, 1993. A copy of the final adoption order or proof of its registration at the Court of Québec, as the case may be, will have to be forwarded with the income tax return of the taxpayer claiming the tax credit.

If you are self-employed in Québec, you will need to add self-employed Québec Pension Plan (QPP) premiums to your Québec tax liability [flowchart box 13Q] and remit this amount to the province, instead of remitting self-employed CPP premiums to the federal government as you would in the case of the other provinces and territories [flowchart box 13]. The premiums under both QPP and CPP are the same.

"Premier toit" tax credit on the first-time purchase of a home

A new refundable tax credit related to the first-time purchase of a home was introduced in December 1994 and modified in May 1995. This credit includes two parts. The first concerns the first-time purchase of a new home, while the second concerns the renovation of a newly acquired existing home. At the time of printing this book, the program was expected to end. Indeed, for the credit to apply, the contractor should have accepted an offer for purchase for the dwelling before December 31, 1995 or the deed of sale should be registered before July 1, 1996.

The following are the main aspects of this program that may be renewed in December 1995 (i.e., continued by Québec) for one year (see your tax advisor in this regard). An individual cannot obtain a credit for both aspects at the same time.

• Refundable tax credit for mortgage interest

An individual who resides in Québec on December 31 can claim a refundable tax credit up to $ 4,000 for mortgage interest paid on a new eligible home that has a value of not more than $150,000 ($125,000 outside the Montreal Urban Community). The tax credit will be equal to 20% of the mortgage interest paid in 1994 and 1995 and cannot be more than $2,000 per year.

• Refundable tax credit for renovation expenditures

An individual who resides in Québec on December 31 can claim a refundable tax credit up to $3,000, which corresponds to 10% of eligible expenditures made on renovation of an existing house that has a value of not more than $135, 000 ($110, 000 outside the Montreal Urban Community).

Health services fund contribution

The health services fund contribution is discussed under that heading in the Employees chapter on page 69.

Alternative minimum tax (AMT)

The Québec AMT is calculated at a rate of 20% [flowchart box E★].

★ Refer to Personal Tax flowchart with AMT, page 193.

The adjusted taxable income [flowchart box D★] on which Québec AMT is calculated can also be different, because net income for Québec tax purposes may be different from federal net income.

To ensure that high-income taxpayers are required to contribute to the financing of public expenditures on the basis of their ability to pay, the strategic investments for the Québec economy account has been eliminated as of the 1994 taxation year. Thus, a taxpayer who formerly benefited from preferential tax treatment in Québec will have to include all of his or her strategic investments when determining whether or not he or she is subject to the alternative minimum tax. However, individual deductions included in this account will continue to be eligible deductions in the determination of a taxpayer's taxable income.

Québec surtaxes

In Québec, a surtax equal to 5% of the provincial tax that exceeds $5,000 and another 5% of the tax that exceeds $10,000 must be added.

However, Québec has a tax reduction (applicable as of the 1994 taxation year) equal to 2% of the excess of $10,000 over tax payable after deducting non-refundable tax credits.

Gifts of works of art to charitable organizations

A tax credit or deduction will not be available for a gift of a work of art to a charitable organization, unless the work of art is sold by the charitable organization within five years. This change is to ensure that the tax advantages that a donor may obtain are those envisaged by the legislation. The measure will not apply to a work of art acquired by a charitable organization as part of its primary mission. It applies to gifts of works of art made after May 9, 1995.

Filing Returns and Paying Your Taxes

203

Filing Returns and Paying Your Taxes

What's new?

- The rate of interest charged on overdue taxes to increase by an additional two percent (proposed).

- Deferral of tax on business income to be eliminated (proposed).

- The filing deadline for individuals reporting business income to be extended to June 15 (proposed).

You can save time, money, and aggravation by being careful about how and when you file and pay your taxes, and how you deal with Revenue Canada. This chapter will help you handle these matters effectively, before you file, when you file and after you file your tax return.

One of the easiest ways to save money is to observe Revenue Canada's payment and filing requirements. Interest and penalties can leave you with a significant and avoidable bill. Daily compounding can quickly double your tax liability. There is little point in conscientious tax planning if you fail to file or pay your taxes on time.

Tax Tip 86

The interest provisions are a two-way street: refunds due to you from Revenue Canada as a result of overpayments of tax will earn interest, although to a much lesser degree than they used to. You begin to accrue interest on an overpayment only 45 days after the later of April 30 or the date you actually filed your return. Although filing your return as early as possible won't necessarily earn you any interest from Revenue Canada, you should get your refund cheque sooner. Accordingly, the funds will be available sooner for you to invest or to use for other purposes.

Improving your cash flow

Interest-free loans to the government?

When you filed your income tax return in March or April, were you thrilled to find that you were getting a large refund from Revenue Canada? A tax refund is a mixed blessing; while expecting and getting a cheque in the mail is pleasant, a large tax refund normally indicates that your cash management could be better. In effect, you are making an interest-free loan to the government, because:

• you are making excessive instalment payments; or

• your employer is withholding too much tax.

Instead of having your money to use and invest throughout the year, you have been giving it to Revenue Canada for its use for what could amount to an entire year or more. When you overpay your tax, you don't get your own money back until after you have filed your tax return for a particular year and it is processed. Nor will you earn a year's interest on the money that you've "advanced". As mentioned above, Revenue Canada has an "interest free processing period" that runs 45 days from the later of April 30 and the date the return is filed. That means that if you file your return on time — on April 30 — no interest will be paid on refunds until after June 14. The same treatment applies when you make excessive instalment payments: you won't begin earning interest on an overpayment until 45 days after the overpayment arose.

Steps to take

To a large extent, you can avoid the problem and improve your cash flow.

If you pay your tax by instalments, you should be reviewing your instalment requirements throughout the year. If you made a large, perhaps unexpected, contribution to your RRSP midyear, recalculate your tax liability. It may be significantly lower than the estimate you made in March because of the RRSP contribution. Your instalments for the remainder of the year should be reduced accordingly.

If you are employed, most of your tax liability is likely satisfied through withholdings at source. If you also:

- incur business or investment losses;

- have significant deductible interest expense;

- make RRSP contributions;

- pay deductible alimony or maintenance to a former spouse; or

- have some other deductible expenditures,

consider writing to the Chief of Source Deductions at your local District Taxation Office for a waiver from or reduction in withholdings. If your request is approved, your employer will receive a letter from Revenue Canada authorizing a reduction in the amount of tax withheld from your income. This could increase your cash flow and allow you to use or invest the funds that otherwise would not be available until you get your tax refund.

The rules that employers must follow regarding source deductions have been eased to permit reduced withholdings from employee remuneration. If your employer deducts amounts that are being paid directly into your RRSP, or if you are paying deductible alimony or maintenance payments, your employer may base the tax deductions at source on the net amount, without having to obtain a waiver of withholding letter from Revenue Canada. Note that CPP and UI contributions must still be based on your gross remuneration.

Tax Tip 87

If you are going to be making a lump sum contribution to your RRSP, for example, from a bonus that you have earned, consider asking your employer to make the contribution directly to your RRSP on your behalf. Some numbers will illustrate how attractive this option can be:

Assume that your top marginal rate is 52 percent and that you will be receiving a bonus of $10,000. If the bonus is paid to you, you will receive $4,800 ($10,000 net of $5,200 of tax). You then contribute the $4,800 to your RRSP, generating a refund of $2,496 ($4,800 x 52%) some time after your file your tax return for the year. If you wanted to make an additional RRSP contribution, you might have to borrow the funds, the interest costs on which would not be tax deductible. If instead you direct your employer to make an RRSP contribution on your behalf of all or a portion of the bonus, you would have a larger amount in your RRSP, no interest to pay and little or no tax, depending on whether you contributed the entire bonus.

Before you file

Social Insurance Number

If you lived or worked in Canada during the year and you file an income tax return, you must include your Social Insurance Number (SIN) on your return. You should also indicate your spouse's SIN on your return.

In the past, use of your SIN on information slips such as T3s, T5s, etc. was not mandatory. Now, however, if you are requested to provide your SIN to a person preparing information returns and fail to do so, you may be liable for a fine of $100 each time you do not provide it. If you do not have a SIN, you have 15 days to apply for one from the time you are requested to provide it, and a further 15 days to supply the number.

208 | **Instalment requirements**

If you are earning employment income and have no other major sources of income, the amount of tax withheld at source by your employer will generally leave you with either a small refund or a small balance owing on April 30. If you have other sources of income, however, you may have to make instalments of tax during the year.

Instalments for a particular year are due quarterly, as follows:

No deadlines		Deadline on 15th of month
January	February	**March**
April	May	**June**
July	August	**September**
October	November	**December**

with any final balance due when you file your return. Late or deficient instalments could result in onerous interest and penalty charges (see Interest and penalties, page 211).

You are required to make quarterly payments if the difference between your tax payable and amounts that have been withheld at source is greater than $2,000 in both the current and either of the two preceding years.

Tax payable includes combined federal and provincial income tax. For Québec residents, the threshold amount is $1,200 of federal tax payable after federal tax withholdings.

Revenue Canada notifies individuals required to remit instalments of the amount of each instalment determined on the basis of tax information from prior years.

Individuals who are required to pay quarterly instalments should have received two notices from Revenue Canada in 1995, one in February with the March and June instalments and one in August with the September and December instalments. Here is how Revenue Canada determines the amounts:

- the first two instalments are based on your tax liability from two years ago, i.e., for 1995, each of your first two instalments would be based on one-quarter of your 1993 tax liability;

- the third and fourth payments are based on your liability for the preceding year, i.e., 1994 for 1995 instalments, with an adjustment to ensure that the total of the four instalments equals your prior year's liability.

If you choose to follow this new method and pay the exact amounts specified by Revenue Canada on time, you will not be charged interest and penalties even if your instalments are short.

Of course, the two other existing options are also available to you if you prefer to continue with the method you have used in the past:

- divide your prior year's tax liability by four and pay that amount each quarter; or

- if you are confident that your current year's liability will be less than that of the previous year, estimate the liability and pay 25% of that amount each quarter. In this case, review your situation before each payment to make sure that your original estimate is still valid.

If you choose this latter option and you estimate incorrectly, interest may be charged on the deficient instalments.

Tax Tip 88

Interest charges on late or deficient instalments can be significant. You can cure a deficient or late instalment payment by early payment or overpayment of the next instalment. Because interest is levied only to the extent that debit interest exceeds any credit offset, you should be able to reduce or eliminate interest charges on late or deficient instalments.

The 1995 federal budget proposes to increase the rate of interest charged on overdue taxes (see page 211, Interest and penalties). For purposes of the interest offset, the same rate of interest will apply to overpayments and underpayments. Accordingly, the new higher interest rate will be charged only on net deficient instalments.

When you file

Filing on the most favourable basis

Tax laws and regulations are not always unambiguous. When filing your return you should choose the most favourable, reasonable interpretation. For example, file your current year's return reflecting the results of a favourable court decision. If your position is challenged, possibly because the case you followed is under appeal, you may have to protect the position you have taken by filing a Notice of Objection. This should enable you to sustain the claim if Revenue Canada eventually agrees with the court's decision. If the decision is subsequently overturned, at least you are in the same position you would have been in had you not made the claim. You should only be out-of-pocket to the extent of some interest charges.

Filing returns

Your income tax return each taxation year must generally be filed by April 30 of the following year. Unless a demand is made for your return, the penalty for late filing is based on the amount of tax payable. If you owe tax but cannot pay it on the due date, the late filing penalty will be avoided if you file your return on time. Conversely, you should face no late filing penalty if your tax is paid in full by April 30, even though you do not file the return until later.

Income from an unincorporated business or a partnership is reported in your personal return. The partnership will have to file information with Revenue Canada and provide you with a reporting slip to enclose with your return. If the business or partnership has a non-calendar year end, income from it must be included in your return for the calendar year in which the fiscal year of the business or partnership ends.

The 1995 federal budget proposes to require sole proprietorships, professional corporations that are members of a partnership and certain partnerships to have their fiscal periods end on December 31. This proposed measure, which is effective for fiscal periods ending after 1994, is described in greater detail on page 77.

The federal budget also proposed to extend the annual filing deadline to June 15 for individuals (other than trusts) reporting business income (other than only from limited partnerships). Tax owing will still be payable on April 30 and interest on unpaid taxes will continue to be charged from that date.

Paying your taxes

If you have a balance of tax owing for a particular year, it is due on April 30 of the following year, the same day on which your return must be filed. If you do not pay the balance by April 30, interest will be charged on the outstanding amount (see Interest and penalties, below).

If you are unable to pay taxes owing by April 30, you should include a letter with your return explaining the situation, or contact the Collections Section of your district office. Revenue Canada will generally accommodate a reasonable payment schedule. You may also include postdated cheques with your return. Again, reason should prevail: do not date your cheques two years from the time the payment is due.

After you file

Interest and penalties

To further encourage the prompt payment of unpaid income taxes (including quarterly instalments), the 1995 federal budget proposes to increase the rate of interest charged on overdue taxes yet another two percentage points. Up until the end of June, 1995, the prescribed rate of interest for a calendar quarter was based on the average yield on three-month Treasury Bills sold in the first month of the preceding quarter, plus two percent. Effective July 1, 1995, this rate will become the T-Bill rate plus four percent (see the table on page 77).

This rate applies to overdue income taxes, insufficient instalment payments, unpaid employee source deductions and other amounts withheld at source, unpaid Canada Pension Plan contributions, and unpaid unemployment insurance premiums. (The rate of interest paid on refunds remains unchanged.)

If you file your return late, even if it is only by one day, you will be subject to a late filing penalty equal to 5% of any unpaid tax, plus 1% for each month (to a maximum of 12 months) for which you fail to file the return after the deadline. If you fail to file on time again within a three-year period, the penalty doubles to 10% plus 2% per month of the unpaid amount to a maximum of 20 months.

If you are neglecting to make instalment payments as required, and the amounts are large enough, additional penalties apply to interest in excess of $1,000 owing on late instalments.

You may be fined $100 for each instance you fail to complete all the information required of you on your return. Even a dishonoured cheque will be expensive: Revenue Canada will add $10 to your tax bill for any NSF cheque. Of course, this is in addition to the fee your bank will charge you. In extreme situations, you could be subject to fines of $1,000 to $25,000, or up to 12 months' imprisonment, or both, if you are convicted of an offence under the Income Tax Act.

Failure to pay your taxes on time can become a rather expensive form of financing. Interest, which is also charged on penalties assessed against you but unpaid, is compounded daily. In addition, interest and penalties are not deductible for tax purposes.

Amending returns

What if you have mailed your return and then discovered an error on the return or received additional information that will change your tax liability? You should inform Revenue Canada of the changes, but do not file a corrected return; a letter explaining the situation is all that is required. If you have received a Notice of Assessment, contact your district taxation office; otherwise, contact your regional taxation centre. Always include your SIN when corresponding with Revenue Canada, to help them find your file.

Revenue Canada will generally permit you to amend your return for errors or omissions up to three years after the date of mailing shown on the Notice of Assessment, the same time limit that the government has for reassessing your return. You should note that Revenue Canada will not entertain amending a return because you had a change of heart regarding an optional deduction.

Resolving problems

You will usually receive a Notice of Assessment from Revenue Canada within about eight to 12 weeks of filing your return. Your return may well be assessed exactly as you filed it. Often, however, you will find changes to your return. If you agree with the changes, correction of a calculation error, for example, you should pay any additional tax owing as soon as possible to avoid interest charges.

If you disagree with the way in which your return has been assessed, remember that you are technically bound by the Notice of Assessment unless you object to it. Should you disagree with the Notice of Assessment, you might pursue one of two courses. The simplest course is to contact your district taxation office, by phone or in person. Have your Social Insurance Number handy. In many instances, problems can be readily explained or resolved on the spot.

You may have to follow a more elaborate procedure if:

- you have postponed getting in touch with Revenue Canada;

- significant amounts of money are involved; or

- you feel the matter is quite complex.

In any of these cases, you should consider filing a Notice of Objection to your assessment. A Notice of Objection may be filed on a prescribed form (Form T400A, which you may obtain from your district taxation office). Alternatively, you may initiate the appeal process by setting out the facts and reasons for your objection in a letter to the Chief of Appeals at your local district office or taxation centre. The limit for objection for individuals and testamentary trusts is the later of one year after the balance due day for your return for the year (for example, May 1, 1997 for your 1995 return, which is due April 30, 1996) and 90 days after the mailing date indicated on your assessment.

Revenue Canada is generally under no obligation to entertain any objections you may have to your assessment if you miss the deadline.

Your return will be reviewed and if Revenue Canada agrees with your position, you will receive a revised Notice of Reassessment. If Revenue Canada disagrees, you will receive notification that the assessment stands. Although you may prepare a Notice of Objection yourself, you should consider seeking professional advice, particularly if the amount of tax at stake is significant.

If you still disagree, or if you have not heard from Revenue Canada within 90 days of filing your objection, you may appeal to the courts. However, before proceeding beyond the objection stage, you should talk to your professional advisor. Interest on any unpaid tax continues to accrue during the time your appeal is in process unless you post acceptable security while your objection is still in process. You may also pay the amount in dispute and wait for a possible refund if the matter is resolved in your favour.

If you appeal to the Tax Court of Canada and the amount in dispute is less than $12,000, an informal appeal procedure is available. You may represent yourself or have your lawyer or accountant or other agent represent you. The appeal process should take about six months. If the amount in dispute exceeds $12,000, general court rules apply. You can still represent yourself, but this is not advisable unless you are well versed in both the Income Tax Act and legal procedure.

Further appeals can be made to higher courts: the Federal Court of Appeal and even to the Supreme Court of Canada. The Supreme Court, however, may refuse to grant leave to hear your appeal. Your legal advisor will help you determine whether you have a case, what your chances of success are, and how expensive the whole procedure is likely to be.

Tax Tip 89

Even if your problem has been satisfactorily resolved by phone or in a personal visit to your District Taxation Office, you should note the deadline for filing a Notice of Objection. If you have not received a revised assessment or a Notice of Reassessment by a week or two before the deadline for filing an objection, consider filing a Notice of Objection in any event to protect your position, particularly if substantial amounts are involved.

Post-assessment examination

The Notice of Assessment that Revenue Canada issues is based on a limited review of your return when it is filed. Once the assessment has been issued, your return may be subject to further examination. Two main types of reviews can be carried out after your return has been assessed:

- Information slips received by Revenue Canada from your employer, from banks, and other financial institutions, from the trustee of your RRSP, etc., are matched with your Social Insurance Number to ensure that you have reported all of your employment and investment income.

- The various expenses, deductions, and credits that you claimed may be subject to further review. You may be asked to provide receipts and other documentation to support your claims. Be sure to keep your supporting documents in case your return is selected for review.

Although any return can be selected for detailed examination, the probability increases with the magnitude of the amounts and the nature of income and expense items. In any case, recognize that if you report income from business or property, your return may be selected for a full audit. If you are going to be audited, you will generally be asked to gather all the information that you used to prepare your return and to meet with a Revenue Canada representative. You may bring your professional advisor with you; it is recommended that you do so if your return was prepared by your advisor. The auditor will go through your return with you, examine your supporting documentation and ask questions. As long as you are able to substantiate all of the items on your return, you should not have any problems.

If the auditor proposes any changes to your return and you disagree, you will have to go through the appeal process, beginning with the filing of a Notice of Objection, as described above.

Fairness Package for taxpayers

The Fairness Package is legislation designed to improve the fairness of the tax system for all Canadians. The Fairness Package contains measures aimed at taxpayers who, because of personal misfortune or circumstances beyond their control, are unable to meet filing or payment deadlines or comply with certain rules. Interest or penalties may be waived or cancelled when they result from factors that are beyond your control, for example, when illness prevents you from filing a tax return by the April 30 deadline. Of course, you are expected to have made reasonable efforts to comply with the law, to minimize delays in filing a return, and to remedy the situation as soon as possible.

In the past, if you wanted to claim a refund in respect of a particular taxation year, you had to do so within three years of that year. Now, in certain circumstances, individuals and testamentary trusts may file for refunds for any taxation year after 1984 without regard to the three-year limitation. Refunds may be allowed if an individual or a testamentary trust files a return for the first time or requests a reassessment. In particular, you may be able to obtain a refund or a reduction in taxes owing if:

- your taxes have been overpaid because of the amount of tax withheld at source by your employer;

- you have neglected to claim refundable tax credits; or

- you previously filed your return and then discovered that a deduction to which you were entitled had been missed.

You may not, however, request an increase in deductions such as capital cost allowance, to generate a refund.

The Income Tax Act contains more than 120 elections that let taxpayers select from specified options how the tax laws will apply to their financial affairs for income tax purposes. The fairness legislation gives the Minister discretionary power to allow you to apply to make a late or amended "election" or to revoke an original election for taxation years back to 1985. This discretion is not intended to permit retroactive tax planning. The elections initially eligible for this treatment are set out in an Income Tax Regulation; others will be added as they are identified.

Books and records

You should keep your tax records for at least four years (approximately the period during which Revenue Canada can reassess your return), and preferably longer. If you operate a business, you must keep your tax and business records for at least six years, and even then you may still have to seek permission from Revenue Canada to destroy them.

218 | Directors' tax risks

You should not accept an appointment as a director of a corporation lightly. In addition to the obligations and responsibilities that you take on as a director, you may find that you are financially at risk. As a director, you face two kinds of tax risks. First, you may be liable for income tax on your director's fees even though the corporation withholds tax from the payments you receive. If the corporation cannot satisfy the tax liability in respect of your income, you may be liable. In effect you will be taxed twice. If you have any doubt about the financial security of the corporation, be sure to satisfy yourself that the corporation is handling the withheld taxes properly.

Potentially more onerous than double taxation on your director's fees is your possible liability for corporate income taxes, Canada Pension Plan payments, and Unemployment Insurance contributions.

Directors of corporations may be jointly and severally liable, together with their corporation, for amounts the corporation has failed to withhold and remit to the Receiver General, as well as for any related interest and penalties. Directors' liability also extends to amounts required to be withheld and remitted under the Canada Pension Plan and the Unemployment Insurance Act.

Over the past few years, Revenue Canada has actively prosecuted corporate directors for failure of the corporation to remit payroll deductions. The cases do not reveal any clear-cut threshold of activity a director must undertake to meet the requirements of due diligence. Revenue Canada has basically taken the position that directors may be absolved of personal liability if they are found to have exercised the degree of care, diligence and skill to prevent the failure that a reasonably prudent person would have exercised in comparable circumstances. To protect yourself, you must ensure that the system of withholding and remitting source deductions is well-established and functioning properly. Ignorance of the law does not appear to be a defence.

Tax Tip 90

No action can be initiated against a former director more than two years after he or she ceases to be a director. Accordingly, if you are currently a director, consider resigning if the corporation of which you are a director is in serious trouble. As an added precaution, also consider registering your resignation with the appropriate corporate registry.

⚜ Québec

If you have to deal with Revenue Québec, you should be aware of the following:

Before you file

In Québec, beginning with the September 1994 instalment, tax instalments will be required when the difference between Québec tax payable (net of the reduction) and Québec tax deducted at source exceeds $1,200 for the current year and either of the two preceding years.

After you file

Interest on refunds starts the 46th day after the later of:

- April 30; and

- the date you file your return.

Furthermore, as set out in the table on page 77, the interest rate paid on refunds is significantly lower (4.75% lower for the fourth quarter of 1995) than the interest rate charged on amounts due.

220

• Interest on deficient instalments

If you have neglected to make your Québec instalment payments, an additional interest of 10% per year is applied only if instalments are less than 90% of the required instalments. This interest is added to the normal interest rate on receivables that Revenue Québec charges.

• Resolving problems

Québec follows the same rules as other jurisdictions for resolving problems, except that in Québec:

- The Minister of Revenue has confirmed that it is now possible to file a Notice of Objection by mailing a single copy of a letter to the person in charge of such notices (the "directeur des oppositions").

- If you receive notification that the income tax assessment stands after you have filed your Notice of Objection or if you have not heard from Revenue Québec within 90 days of filing your Notice of Objection, you may appeal to the courts.

  You can appeal successively to:

- the Québec Court (civil division);

- the Québec Court of Appeal; and

- the Supreme Court of Canada.

  An individual can also bring his or her case before the Small Claims Court. Doing so waives the right to any remedy before any other court.

  An individual can also go to the complaints office of Revenue Québec. The brochure entitled *A New Mechanism for Resolving Tax Problems: The Bureau des Plaintes of Revenue Québec* (INF-138) explains how an individual can submit a complaint in writing to this new service of Revenue Québec.

Québec fairness package and new administrative rules

Québec has adopted its Québec Charter of rights, which was published at the back of the 1994 Québec tax return. In addition, the Bill 70 (now 1995, ch. 36) assented to in June 1995, introduced many key changes to the administration of Revenue Québec.

Three changes are particularly noteworthy. Individuals who pay tax in Québec now have the right to request a reduction or cancellation of any interest and penalties, upon satisfying certain criteria (explained in Interpretation Bulletin LMR. 94.1–1R1, dated March 31, 1995). You may want to discuss any request with your professional advisor, who should be able to explain these broad guidelines. In addition, an individual who missed the deadline for filing an objection may be able to have the deadline extended. Finally, an individual may request a refund of overpaid income taxes for taxation years after 1984.

Looking Ahead

Looking Ahead

What's new?

- April 30, 1997 is the deadline for a late-filed capital gains exemption election.

- The family trust preferred beneficiary election is to be eliminated (proposed).

- The 21-year rule for trusts is to be reinstated (proposed).

Your personal tax strategy should include looking into the future. You need to consider your own tax affairs and concerns, as well as anticipated changes in the tax system. This chapter briefly reviews both aspects of looking ahead.

Your own tax affairs

Tax planning is not something that you start to think about in December. With the exception of your RRSP contribution, which you can make within the first 60 days of the next year, all is pretty much said and done by December 31. The earlier in the year that you start your tax planning, the more opportunities you will have to act on some of the ideas in this book and to minimize your tax liability. Although you may not need a great deal of time to put some of these suggestions into place, others will require lead time. Keeping your records organized should allow you to identify opportunities and to minimize the risk of making costly mistakes such as underpaying your instalments.

The rest of 1995 and into 1996

• Dealing with the elimination of the deferral of tax on business income

Tax advisors pleaded with the government to delay the implementation date of the proposed rules requiring that certain business income be reported on a calendar year basis (see page 77). To date, no relief has been announced. Accordingly, you need to ensure that your reporting systems and methods have been modified to comply with the new rules.

Further, if you have an existing business, consider consulting with your professional advisor about whether it is beneficial for you to use the alternative method of computing income. If you decide to use the alternative method, you must make an election to do so by June 15, 1996.

• Lifetime capital gains exemption

The $100,000 lifetime capital gains exemption was eliminated for gains realized or accrued after February 22, 1994. If you still have capital gains exemption available, however, you may be able to take advantage of a special election that will allow you to use some or all of that unused exemption. Although the election was due with your 1994 income tax return, you may still make a late-filed election with your 1995 or 1996 income tax returns (due April 30, 1996 or April 30, 1997 respectively). A penalty must be prepaid with your election for it to be valid (refer to page 107 for further details). If you have capital gains exemption available, owned capital property on February 22, 1994 with accrued gains and do not make the election, the unused exemption will be lost to you forever.

• Eliminating CNIL problems

If you are planning to take advantage of the enhanced lifetime capital gains exemption this year (page 107), ensure that your ability to access the exemption is not reduced or delayed because you have a CNIL. You still have time to restructure borrowings or the ownership of some investments and eliminate your CNIL (see page 138).

Tax Tip 91

If you have CNILs and also are the controlling shareholder of a corporation, consider paying yourself a sufficient dividend to cure your CNIL problem.

Your CNIL account at the end of 1994 is relevant if you are planning to make a late-filed election for the unused portion of the $100,000 lifetime capital gains exemption. Unfortunately, it is too late for a cure: you may lose all or a portion of the unused exemption if you had a CNIL on December 31, 1994 (your CNIL after that date will affect only the enhanced capital gains exemption). Accordingly, you should carefully review your investment income and expenses to ensure that your CNIL account is accurate up to December 31, 1994. In particular, make sure you have not missed any investment income.

• Reviewing your instalment payments

Review your tax position prior to making the third and final instalments for the year to ensure that you are not offside. If you find that your tax liability will be larger than expected, you should consider increasing your payments, unless you have chosen to make your instalments based on Revenue Canada's instalment requirements (see page 208).

• Spousal RRSPs

Making a contribution to a spousal RRSP based on your own contribution entitlement is still one of the most effective ways of income splitting.

• Salary/dividend mix

If you are a controlling shareholder of a private company, you are likely in a position to decide what type of compensation you will receive. In choosing between salary and dividends, you should ensure that you are receiving at least enough salary to permit you to make maximum contributions to your RRSP (see page 39).

Tax Tip 92

Your RRSP contribution limit in 1996 will be based on 1995 earned income. To make the maximum contribution next year, you will need $80,556 of earned income in 1995.

• Pension income credit

If you are age 65 or over and are not taking advantage of the pension income credit, consider arranging to receive eligible pension income, perhaps by converting a portion of your RRSP to a retirement income stream that will provide you with at least $1,000 of eligible pension income (see page 150).

• "Junior" tax returns

When you are in the midst of preparing to file your income tax returns, consider encouraging your children who are over age 18 (or younger if they have sufficient income) to file their own income tax returns. University students often fail to file tax returns, since the credit for tuition fees offsets tax that would be payable on any income earned (or the tuition fee credit may have been transferred to you as a supporting person). The child is foregoing credits to which he or she may be entitled by not filing a return. Further, the financial benefits are not the only reason that young adults should be filing their own returns. There are probably many young adults who have their own credit cards, yet know little about the procedures and consequences involved in filing an income tax return. This would be an excellent opportunity to begin to shift the burden of responsibility to these young adults for their own financial affairs.

Tax Tip 93

Young adults age 19 or over may claim their own GST credit (even if they have no income), as well as any provincial credits that may be available and that can be claimed only by filing an income tax return.

• Home Buyers' Plan

The Home Buyers' Plan, originally introduced as a temporary measure to allow individuals to use existing funds in their RRSPs to purchase a home, continues to apply for first-time home buyers only.

You may not participate in the ongoing version of the Home Buyers' Plan if you or your spouse withdrew funds under the original Home Buyers' Plan that was scheduled to expire on March 2, 1994. If you applied to participate before that date and you actually received the funds prior to April 1994, you are subject to the rules under the original plan.

You are considered to be a first-time home buyer if neither you nor your spouse, during your marriage, owned a home and lived in it as your principal place of residence at any time in the period beginning on January 1 of the fourth calendar year before the withdrawal and ending on the 31st day before the withdrawal from your RRSP. Further, you may participate in the Home Buyers' Plan only once.

A qualifying home must be located in Canada and cannot have been previously owned by you or your spouse. You must intend to occupy it as your principal place of residence no later than one year after its acquisition. Both new and existing homes are eligible and all types of structures are included in the definition: a detached house; a semi-detached house; a townhouse; a condominium; a mobile home; an apartment in a duplex, triplex, fourplex or apartment building; and even a share in a co-operative housing corporation.

You may withdraw up to $20,000 from your RRSP (up to $40,000 per couple) free of tax. You may acquire a qualifying home either on your own or jointly with one or more other persons. A husband and wife may each withdraw $20,000 from their own RRSPs as long as they own the home jointly. If you contributed $20,000 to your own plan and $20,000 to your spouse's plan, you may each withdraw $20,000 to jointly acquire a home. If you did not contribute to your own plan, but contributed $40,000 to a spousal plan, your spouse can withdraw no more than $20,000, even if you are acquiring the property jointly.

You must repay your RRSP the funds withdrawn for this purpose in at least 15 annual equal instalments. If you withdraw funds from your RRSP after March 1, 1994, the 15-year repayment period will begin in the second calendar year following the year in which the withdrawal is made. In addition, you must purchase a qualifying home before October 1 of the calendar year following the year of withdrawal. For example, if you made a Home Buyers' Plan withdrawal of $15,000 on April 15, 1995, you have until October 1, 1996 to acquire a qualifying home and your first annual repayment of $1,000 will be due by the end of 1997. You may elect to have a repayment made in the first 60 days of a year treated as having been made in the preceding year. Of course, if you repay more than the minimum amount in a particular year, in the following year your payment would be based on the amount left to be repaid, divided by the number of years left in the 15-year repayment period. If you fail to meet the repayment schedule or fall short of a payment in a particular year, the unrepaid amount will be added to your income and, accordingly, will be subject to tax at your marginal tax rate.

To request a withdrawal from your RRSP under the Home Buyers' Plan, you must complete a prescribed form (T1036). The form details the location of the qualifying home and confirms that you intend to use that home as your principal place of residence no later than one year after its acquisition. Prior to receiving funds from your RRSP, you must have entered into an agreement in writing for the acquisition or construction of the qualifying home.

If you withdraw funds in accordance with the Home Buyers' Plan but the purchase doesn't go through for some reason, you won't be penalized with an income inclusion, provided that you return the funds to your RRSP by the end of the following year.

You will not be able to claim a tax deduction for contributions to your RRSP that are withdrawn within 90 days under the Home Buyers' Plan. For purposes of this rule, contributions to your RRSP within the 90-day period will not be considered to be withdrawn except to the extent that the RRSP balance after the withdrawals is less than the amount of such contributions. Of course, your RRSP room in that period will not be lost; you will be able to carry it forward for use in future years (see page 39).

The longer term: estate planning

Two common misconceptions are associated with the term estate planning: the first is that it is something to be worried about sometime in the future when you are "older"; the second is that significant amounts of money must be involved. The fact is that while you may not have a formal estate plan in mind at the tender age of 21, everyone over the age of majority should give some thought to the consequences of their death, particularly if there are any dependants. You should, however, be wary of carrying out plans for the transfer of your wealth until your own position is secure and you are confident of the ability of your intended beneficiaries to deal with the implications.

An estate plan can be as simple or as elaborate as you wish. Your circumstances and financial situation will, of course, affect the complexity of your estate plan. The size of your estate should not be an issue either: we are all concerned with ensuring that we will be able to maintain our life-styles after retirement, that our dependants will be taken care of in the event of our death, and that our assets will be distributed on our death according to our wishes.

Estate planning is not something that you do once and for all. Rather, it should be a continuing process of evaluating your personal and business circumstances and directing the manner in which your assets are preserved and ultimately distributed.

To remain effective, your estate plan should be reviewed periodically and revised to accommodate changes in your financial and personal life or in legislation, including taxation.

• Insurance

Choosing the appropriate insurance program may satisfy a variety of objectives. The most important one is to provide your spouse and children with a replacement for the income that is lost on your death and to provide them with the funds necessary to cover the payment of income taxes and other debts and expenses arising on death. Some forms of life insurance policies are looked on as investments as well

as providing protection. An exempt life insurance policy provides an **231**
opportunity to accommodate investment on a favourable tax basis. As
with other investments, tax consequences should not be the primary
concern in evaluating the opportunity and rates of return should be
carefully considered. However, the low rate of tax applicable to
exempt policy earnings and the possibility of receiving the benefit of
the policy free of tax (during life as well as on death) may make this a
worthwhile option in some circumstances. Your professional advisors
can tell you what types of whole life insurance policies are exempt.

In business situations, insurance may be used to provide funding
for the eventual purchase of assets or shares in connection with a buy-
out of partners or partners' heirs.

Insurance proceeds that are payable as a result of the death of the
insured are not taxable in the hands of the beneficiary.

• Up-to-date wills

Dying intestate (without a will) can defeat almost all the estate planning arrangements you have worked hard to put into place. Provincial
laws dictate how your assets are to be divided if you do not have a
will.

Tax Tip 94

Both you and your spouse should have a will. This is probably
one of the most critical elements of your estate planning program.

Your will should be reviewed at least every five years by your
lawyer and also by your professional tax advisor if your affairs have
become at all complex. Your lawyer will suggest any necessary changes.
It should also be reassessed in light of changes in the law, particularly
family law. In some provinces, the law virtually dictates how family
assets are to be divided even if you have drafted a comprehensive
will. It should certainly be reviewed if your personal or financial circumstances have changed. For example, your will is invalid if you

subsequently become divorced. Your will should be reviewed if you get married, if you adopt a child, if one of your beneficiaries dies, and even if you make a large tax-free transfer to your RRSP.

• Charitable donations

Charitable gifts may be made during your lifetime or through your will. There are various ways that you may achieve your donative objectives: a bequest of cash to your favourite charity is by no means your only option.

A bequest made in a will is treated as though the gift were made immediately before death. Accordingly, a tax credit for a testamentary donation will be available on your final tax return. As discussed on page 188, donations claimed in any one year cannot exceed 20 percent of net income. Excess donations in the year of death may be carried back and used in the previous year, subject of course, to the 20 percent net income limitation.

In addition to gifts of cash, you may specify that donations be made of other types of property that you may own. For example, gifts in kind, gifts of life insurance, gifts of cultural property and gifts to the Crown.

Gifts in kind involve property, including shares, bonds, real estate and artwork. Although a cash gift simply results in a tax credit, a gift in kind has a further effect on your tax return. When you make a gift of property, you are normally deemed to have disposed of the property at its fair market value and to have made a gift of an equal amount. Your tax credit will be based on the fair market value of the property and will be treated the same way as if it were a gift of cash. You must also recognize any capital gain or income on the deemed disposition, i.e., as if the property had been sold.

Special rules that allow some planning flexibility apply to gifts in kind. If the property that you are gifting has appreciated in value, you may elect an amount that falls between the fair market value and the adjusted cost base of the property to be the deemed proceeds of disposition and the amount of your gift. In this way, you can control the amount of the capital gain or income that must be realized on your return, as well as the amount of the gift. This may be particularly important if the gift would otherwise exceed the 20 percent of net income limitation or if you have capital losses against which capital gains on the deemed disposition would be offset.

Gifts to the Crown include gifts to the federal or provincial governments as well as to certain government agencies. Universities and hospitals in some provinces have established foundations that also qualify as Crown agencies. Gifts to the Crown are not subject to the 20 percent net income limitation.

Gifts of cultural property are not subject to the 20 percent limitation either. Such donations must, however, be made to institutions or public authorities designated as such under the Cultural Property Export and Import Act. Further, the property must be an object that the Canadian Cultural Property Export Review Board has determined meets certain criteria.

You may also consider donating a whole life insurance policy to your favourite charity. To accomplish this, you would transfer the policy to the charity and have the charity become the registered beneficiary. The cash surrender value of the policy will be the amount of your donation for tax purposes. Accumulated dividends and interest will increase the value; any policy loan outstanding will decrease it. If the value of the policy exceeds the cost of it to you, you must recognize the excess as though you cashed it in. Further, if you continue to pay premiums on the policy, the payments will be considered to be additional charitable donations eligible for the tax credit.

There are many ways to ensure that your wishes are carried out. You may begin a system of planned giving today, or you may decide that your will is the vehicle through which you will distribute your assets. In any event, consider discussing your objectives and concerns with your professional advisor, particularly if significant assets are concerned and where provincial family law may have a significant effect on your estate plan.

• Estate freezing

In many ways, estate freezing is an extension of income splitting. The idea behind this type of planning is to transfer any future growth in the value of an asset (and any tax liability on future appreciation) to your heirs. Ideally, however, you would retain control over the asset during your lifetime. In an estate freeze, the value of an asset to you is frozen for tax purposes. In so doing, an immediate tax liability could result because you may have to recognize a capital gain when ownership of the asset is transferred. To the extent that you have not exhausted it, however, the capital gain could be eligible for the enhanced $400,000 capital gains exemption. Even if the exemption is not available, other deferral methods are.

Estate freezes are often executed using a corporation, rather than through a direct sale or transfer to an intended beneficiary. Tax can be deferred, minimized or even eliminated. Ownership of the shares in the corporation should be structured so as to ensure that growth in the value of assets accrues to your heirs, while you retain control over the corporation, and accordingly over the assets, during your lifetime. Generally, personal assets can be transferred into a corporation with no immediate tax consequences, the corporation being considered to acquire the assets at your cost.

Estate freezing is complex. You should discuss any ideas or concerns you might have with your professional tax advisor.

• Family trusts

A trust is an arrangement that offers enormous flexibility in structuring your affairs and controlling the use of your property. A trust is treated as separate person for income tax purposes; indeed a trust is taxed much like an individual (personal tax credits, however, are not available to a trust).

A testamentary trust, basically a trust created under your will, is taxed at the same rates as those that apply to individuals. An *inter vivos* trust on the other hand (one that you set up today) is taxed at the top rate of tax for individuals.

Family trusts, which may be either *inter vivos* or testamentary trusts, are used for a variety of purposes. For example, to achieve income splitting (although the attribution rules limit the opportunities); to provide for the maintenance and education of infants; to provide maintenance and care for a child with a disability; to centralize and preserve control of business interests; to provide financial independence for children who have reached the age of majority, while at the same time controlling the time at which the child will obtain control over the property in question; or to provide for the children of a former marriage. These are but a few of the many other reasons for establishing a family trust.

Trust assets are generally made subject to capital gains tax by being deemed to be disposed of every 21 years. Trusts are currently permitted to file an election to defer that deemed disposition until the death of the last "exempt beneficiary" under the trust. The 1995 federal budget proposes to eliminate that election effective January 1, 1999. Trusts that had filed the election will be subject to a deemed disposition of trust assets at fair market value on January 1, 1999.

As well, a preferred beneficiary election allows trust income to be allocated to certain close beneficiaries of the trust. That income is then taxed in their hands, rather than at the trust level, even though the income might never be distributed to those beneficiaries. The 1995 federal budget proposes to eliminate the income-splitting and other tax benefits of these elections for taxation years of trusts that commence after 1995. They will continue to be permitted, however, for individuals entitled to a tax credit for mental or physical impairment.

Tax Tip 95

If you currently have (or planned to establish shortly) a family trust in respect of which an election to defer the 21-year deemed disposition has been made (or will be made), or if you have been making a preferred beneficiary election, you should discuss the ramifications of the budget proposals with your professional advisor. They could be significant.

• Offshore protection trusts

Offshore protection trusts are becoming increasingly popular vehicles for affluent individuals who might be exposed to personal liability in a potential lawsuit. If your situation is such that you might become at risk, you might look to transferring assets offshore to jurisdictions like the Bahamas, the Channel Islands, the Cayman Islands, or other such exotic havens, to protect your assets from the claims of creditors in Canada.

The idea is that if assets are held in a jurisdiction where a Canadian judgment is not recognized (or even where the domestic judgment is enforceable), the cost and difficulty associated with taking action in a foreign court would discourage a creditor from pursuing the matter.

When you are setting up the trust, there must be no claims or potential claims in the offing. You must be solvent, and must have no intent to defraud any of your creditors at the time of setting up your protective offshore trust.

For an offshore protection trust arrangement to make sense, an individual should have at least half a million dollars of liquid and easily movable assets available for transfer. Of course, there are fees associated with setting up the trust, as well as annual administration costs.

A final caveat: the use of an offshore trust may help you protect your assets, but it won't help you escape Revenue Canada. Canadian residents are taxable on their worldwide income. Accordingly, any income that is earned on assets in the offshore trust will still be taxable in your hands.

• Taxes on death

There are no federal or provincial death taxes per se in Canada. Generally, however, you are deemed to have disposed of all of your capital property immediately prior to death for proceeds equal to the fair market value of the assets at that time. Any capital gains that have accrued to the date of death would be included and taxed in your final income tax return, with one major exception: unless you elect otherwise, all assets passing to your spouse or a spousal trust are transferred at cost, with the spouse or spousal trust inheriting your cost base. Accordingly, no immediate income tax consequences result. Assets passing to anyone else, including a trust, are subject to the deemed disposition rules.

Tax Tip 96

To the extent that it has not been exhausted, the enhanced $400,000 capital gains exemption may shelter any capital gains arising on qualified small business corporation shares or qualified farm property as a result of the deemed disposition rules. In addition, the AMT provisions are not applicable in the year of death.

The executors of your estate will be responsible for payment of any taxes owing on your final income tax return and for taxes payable on income earned on your assets before they are distributed to your beneficiaries.

Tax Tip 97

In addition to a final return of income, the executor of an estate may choose to file up to three additional separate returns in respect of certain types of income that have been earned but unrealized at the date of death. Full personal tax credits may be claimed for each of the separate returns, which could result in substantial tax savings.

Changes to the tax system

Changes to the tax system result from changes in federal and provincial legislation and regulations, new interpretations resulting from court

238

decisions, and administrative changes by Revenue Canada. Changes to federal legislation can be made through federal budgets, as well as technical amendment bills. Technical amendment bills tend to be somewhat predictable.

Court decisions are less predictable, but important new interpretations are usually reported in the popular press. Revenue Canada can change its interpretation at any time through press releases, interpretation bulletins, and information circulars.

This book reflects changes in income tax to October 31, 1995 and includes tax laws that have been passed up to that date, as well as changes proposed in the 1995 federal budget. Provincial governments generally present their budgets in late winter or spring. Of course, governments can deviate from this pattern and may bring down budgets at any time. When *Personal Tax Strategy* was written, all the provinces and territories had brought down their 1995-96 budgets. Personal income tax changes introduced in those budgets are reflected in this book.

Income taxes for the provinces and territories (other than Québec, which collects its own tax) are currently calculated as a percentage of federal rates; the federal government collects income taxes on their behalf. Apparently, there is a possibility that the provinces and territories may be permitted to set provincial tax regimes independent of federal rates and to collect those taxes themselves. This could lead to a more complex array of income taxes across Canada, although for most individuals the most visible change would likely be the requirement to file separate federal and provincial/territorial income tax returns.

Technical amendments can be extremely important for a few taxpayers, and insignificant to others, although some technical amendments have broader application. Your professional advisor can help you determine whether this year's technical amendments affect you.

Appendices

This appendix will help you:
- determine your 1995 marginal tax rate
- compare tax rates in Canada

Appendix 1
Combined marginal rates

What Are Combined Marginal Rates?

Combined marginal rates are the total of federal marginal rates (Appendix 4) and provincial marginal rates (Appendix 5), including federal and provincial surtaxes. In this appendix, the rates take into account any provincial tax reductions and the Northwest Territories' Cost of Living Tax Credit.

The combined marginal rates shown in this appendix apply to most income, such as salaries and bank interest. Appendix 3 shows top marginal rates for certain **investment income.**

Your marginal rate is the highest marginal rate that applies to you, because it is the percentage of any additional taxable income that you will pay as income tax. If your marginal rate is 49%, then 49% of the last dollar you earned, and of any additional income you earn, will go to pay income taxes.

Your marginal rate also measures the value of any deduction from taxable income. At a 49% marginal rate, a $100 deduction reduces your tax bill by $49.

The rates shown here **include the provincial tax reductions** that Alberta, British Columbia, Manitoba, Nova Scotia, Ontario, Saskatchewan and Québec have. Except for Québec, the reductions normally affect only taxpayers in the lowest income brackets. Reductions are discussed in Appendix 5.

Top marginal rates are in bold type toward the right of the table. (Top marginal rates are also shown in Appendices 2 and 3.)

To see how your marginal rate derives from federal and provincial taxes and surtaxes, refer to Appendices 4 and 5.

Reading the Charts

The charts on pages 241, 253, 257 and 258 show a range of **taxable income**, starting at zero on the left, and

1995 Combined marginal rates (including all surtaxes)

For help on reading this chart, see *Reading the Charts* on page 242.

A1

Taxable income →

Provincial tax as % of basic federal tax		$0	$6,456	$29,590	$59,180	$62,195			Top Marginal Rate
52.5%	British Columbia*	17.51%*	26.44% / 28.44%*	26.44%	40.43%	44.53%	51.11%		54.16%
58%	Ontario*	17.51%* / 47.09%*	27.37%	41.86%	44.88%	51.50% / 50.05%	49.66%		53.19%
n/a	Québec	14.71% / 34.09%*	36.13%*	38.17%*	45.95%* / 47.12%*	48.19%*	51.49%		52.94%
50%	Saskatchewan*	17.51%* / 34.06%* / 29.06%	29.06%	43.28%	45.53%	48.89%	50.50%		51.95%
64%	New Brunswick	28.39%		43.42%	48.43%	49.88%			51.36%
69%	Newfoundland	0%	29.24%	44.72%	49.88%				51.33%
52%	Manitoba*	17.51%*	30.35%*	28.35%	44.30%	48.95%			50.40%
59.5%	Nova Scotia*	17.51%* / 0%	27.63% / 32.63%	27.63%	42.30% / 42.25%	47.13%	48.58%		50.30%
59.5%	Prince Edward Island	27.63%		42.25%	47.13%	48.58%			50.30%
50%	Yukon	26.01%		39.78%	44.37%	45.10%			46.55%
52%	Non-resident	0%	26.35%	40.30%	44.95%				46.40%
45.5%	Alberta*	17.51%*	29.86%*	25.75%	39.11%	40.06%	44.62%		46.07%
45%	Northwest Territories**	-1.25%	23.91%**	24.16%**	37.48%	37.73%** / 42.17%**	43.62%**		44.37%

Highest Top Marginal Rate → Lowest Top Marginal Rate

Taxable income → $0 $10,000 $20,000 $30,000 $40,000 $50,000 $60,000 $70,000 $80,000 $90,000 $100,000

* Provincial tax reductions in Alberta, British Columbia, Manitoba, Nova Scotia, Ontario, and Saskatchewan will alter the marginal rates for low-income taxpayers. Québec taxpayers with taxable incomes up to about $53,000 are affected. Brackets affected by or created by tax reductions are marked by broken lines.

** The results reflect the Northwest Territories' Cost of Living Tax Credit, which reduces tax payable and creates additional brackets.

241

Appendix 1
Combined marginal rates

ending at an amount over $100,000. (Above that level no additional tax brackets exist, so you can imagine the bars continuing indefinitely to the right.) Taxable income is drawn to scale.

Taxable income is your income from all sources, less certain deductions (see page 180).

The jurisdictions are in descending order: British Columbia has the highest top marginal rate, (54.16%) for 1995, so it appears first. The Northwest Territories, with the lowest top marginal rate (44.37%), appears last. This arrangement, with taxable income drawn to scale and provinces listed in order of decreasing top marginal rate, is used in most of the appendices to *Personal Tax Strategy*.

To find your marginal tax rate on page 241, or other data on pages 253, 257 or 258, simply look for the jurisdiction in which you reside. (Rates for non-residents are also given.) Then move across the chart to the box that corresponds to your taxable income.

As explained in Appendix 5, except for Québec, provincial income taxes before surtaxes are simply a proportion of basic federal tax. Each jurisdiction sets its own proportion. This proportion (or factor) is shown at the left of the table.

Appendix 2
How much tax?

This appendix will help you:
• estimate your 1995 income tax
• compare taxes across
  Canada

The big question is always: How much tax?

Assumptions

The table shows the total income tax payable by a person whose only tax credit is the basic non-refundable personal credit and who has no income from Canadian dividends. Amounts shown **include all surtaxes, provincial tax reductions, and the Northwest Territories' Cost of Living Tax Credit** (see Appendices 1, 4 and 5).

The table should be read with care. If you have tax credits other than the basic personal credit, or if your income includes Canadian dividends, your tax will be lower than the amount shown.

Effective rates

An **effective rate of tax** (total tax as a percentage of taxable income) is also given in the table. Effective rates are average tax rates [unlike marginal rates, which apply to incremental income.] (see Appendix 1).

The column at the extreme right repeats the **top marginal rates** that appear in Appendices 1 and 3. As taxable income gets larger, the effective rate approaches the marginal rate, so this column also represents the effective rate for an infinite (!) taxable income.

You can **estimate your income tax liability** in several ways. For example:

• multiply your taxable income by an effective rate interpolated from those in the table on page 245;

or

• interpolate the amount of tax from those in the table on page 245; or

• use the tax tables on pages 246 and 247.

1995 Income tax payable and effective rates

	Taxable Income										
	$10,000	$25,000	$50,000	$100,000	$150,000	$200,000	$250,000	$300,000	$500,000	$1,000,000	Top rate
British Columbia	$890 8.87%	$4,900 19.61%	$14,400 28.73%	$39,800 39.80%	$66,900 44.59%	$94,000 46.98%	$121,000 48.42%	$148,100 49.37%	$256,400 51.29%	$327,200 52.72%	54.16%
Ontario	$970 9.70%	$5,080 20.30%	$14,900 29.75%	$40,500 40.51%	$67,100 44.73%	$93,700 46.85%	$120,300 48.11%	$146,900 48.96%	$253,300 50.65%	$319,200 51.92%	53.19%
Québec	$840 8.41%	$6,220 24.88%	$17,600 35.13%	$43,600 43.60%	$70,100 46.71%	$96,500 48.27%	$123,000 49.20%	$149,500 49.82%	$255,300 51.07%	$520,000 52.00%	52.94%
Saskatchewan	$960 9.62%	$5,520 22.09%	$15,900 31.86%	$41,300 41.27%	$67,200 44.83%	$93,200 46.61%	$119,200 47.68%	$145,200 48.39%	$249,100 49.81%	$508,800 50.88%	51.95%
New Brunswick	$1,010 10.06%	$5,260 21.06%	$15,400 30.86%	$39,900 39.85%	$65,900 43.69%	$91,200 45.61%	$116,900 46.76%	$142,600 47.53%	$245,300 49.06%	$502,100 50.21%	51.36%
Newfoundland	$1,040 10.36%	$5,420 21.69%	$15,900 31.78%	$40,900 40.91%	$66,600 44.38%	$92,200 46.12%	$117,900 47.16%	$143,600 47.86%	$246,200 49.25%	$502,900 50.29%	51.33%
Manitoba	$900 9.04%	$5,390 21.55%	$15,700 31.44%	$40,300 40.32%	$65,500 43.68%	$90,700 45.36%	$115,900 46.37%	$141,100 47.04%	$241,900 48.38%	$493,900 49.39%	50.40%
Nova Scotia	$780 7.79%	$5,120 20.49%	$15,000 30.03%	$39,100 39.07%	$64,200 42.82%	$89,400 44.69%	$114,500 45.81%	$139,700 46.56%	$240,300 48.06%	$491,800 49.18%	50.30%
Prince Edward Island	$980 9.79%	$5,120 20.49%	$15,000 30.03%	$38,800 38.82%	$64,000 42.65%	$89,100 44.56%	$114,300 45.71%	$139,400 46.47%	$240,000 48.01%	$491,500 49.15%	50.30%
Yukon	$920 9.22%	$4,820 19.29%	$14,100 28.27%	$36,700 36.73%	$60,000 40.00%	$83,300 41.64%	$106,600 42.62%	$129,800 43.27%	$222,900 44.58%	$455,600 45.56%	46.55%
Non-resident	$930 9.34%	$4,890 19.55%	$14,300 28.64%	$36,900 36.92%	$60,100 40.08%	$83,300 41.66%	$106,500 42.61%	$129,700 43.24%	$222,500 44.50%	$454,500 45.45%	46.40%
Alberta	$680.00 6.77%	$4,810 19.23%	$14,000 28.05%	$36,500 36.47%	$59,500 39.67%	$82,500 41.27%	$105,600 42.23%	$128,600 42.87%	$220,700 44.15%	$451,100 45.11%	46.07%
Northwest Territories	$770.00 7.67%	$4,390 17.54%	$13,100 26.30%	$34,600 34.63%	$56,800 37.88%	$79,000 39.50%	$101,200 40.47%	$123,400 41.12%	$212,100 42.42%	$434,000 43.40%	44.37%

Highest Top Marginal Rate (top) ... Lowest Top Marginal Rate (bottom)

Tax is rounded to the nearest $10 in the first two columns, and to the $100 in the others. Effective rates are rounded to the nearest hundredth of a percent.

Because Québec has a different system of calculating provincial tax, comparisons must be made with care. Allowable deductions in Québec will generally yield a lower taxable income than residents elsewhere in Canada would have, given the same total income.

Alberta

Bracket	$Tax	+ % of excess
$62,193	$19,048	46.07%
$59,180	$17,704	44.62%
$44,050	$11,643	40.06%
$29,590	$5,988	39.11%
$16,507	$2,620	25.75%
$9,545	$541	29.86%
$6,456	$0	17.51%
$0	$0	0.00%

British Columbia

Bracket	$Tax	+ % of excess
$78,203	$27,999	54.16%
$62,193	$19,816	51.11%
$59,180	$18,320	49.66%
$53,292	$15,698	44.53%
$29,590	$6,115	40.43%
$17,500	$2,919	26.44%
$15,000	$2,209	28.44%
$7,016	$98	26.44%
$6,456	$0	17.51%
$0	$0	0.00%

Manitoba

Bracket	$Tax	+ % of excess
$62,193	$21,263	50.40%
$59,180	$19,788	48.95%
$30,000	$6,861	44.30%
$29,590	$6,688	42.30%
$21,500	$4,394	28.35%
$7,794	$234	30.35%
$6,456	$0	17.51%
$0	$0	0.00%

New Brunswick

Bracket	$Tax	+ % of excess
$91,827	$35,656	51.36%
$62,193	$20,875	49.88%
$59,180	$19,416	48.43%
$29,590	$6,568	43.42%
$6,456	$0	28.39%
$0	$0	0.00%

Newfoundland

Bracket	$Tax	+ % of excess
$62,193	$21,500	51.33%
$59,180	$19,997	49.88%
$29,590	$6,764	44.72%
$6,456	$0	29.24%
$0	$0	0.00%

Nova Scotia

Bracket	$Tax	+ % of excess
$77,044	$27,526	50.30%
$62,193	$20,313	48.58%
$59,180	$18,893	47.13%
$29,590	$6,391	42.25%
$19,000	$3,465	27.63%
$15,000	$2,160	32.63%
$8,433	$346	27.63%
$6,456	$0	17.51%
$0	$0	0.00%

Non-residents

Bracket	$Tax	+ % of excess
$62,193	$19,375	46.40%
$59,180	$18,021	44.95%
$29,590	$6,096	40.30%
$6,456	$0	26.35%
$0	$0	0.00%

Ontario

Bracket	$Tax	+ % of excess
$66,652	$22,772	53.19%
$62,193	$20,475	51.50%
$59,180	$18,967	50.05%
$50,936	$15,267	44.88%
$29,590	$6,332	41.86%
$9,575	$854	27.37%
$8,535	$364	47.09%
$6,456	$0	17.51%
$0	$0	0.00%

Prince Edward Island

Bracket	$Tax	+% of excess
$91,532	$34,564	50.30%
$62,193	$20,313	48.58%
$59,180	$18,893	47.13%
$29,590	$6,391	42.25%
$6,456	$0	27.63%
$0	$0	0.00%

Québec

Bracket	$Tax	+% of excess
$62,193	$23,593	52.94%
$59,180	$22,042	51.49%
$52,625	$18,837	48.89%
$50,000	$17,572	48.19%
$31,000	$8,619	47.12%
$29,590	$7,971	45.95%
$23,000	$5,456	38.17%
$14,000	$2,205	36.13%
$8,348	$278	34.09%
$6,456	$0	14.71%
$0	$0	0.00%

Northwest Territories

Bracket	$Tax	+% of excess
$66,000	$19,544	44.37%
$62,193	$17,884	43.62%
$59,180	$16,613	42.17%
$48,000	$12,395	37.73%
$29,590	$5,495	37.48%
$12,000	$1,245	24.16%
$6,456	($81)	23.91%
$0	$0	-1.25%

Saskatchewan

Bracket	$Tax	+% of excess
$62,193	$21,502	51.95%
$59,180	$19,980	50.50%
$39,202	$10,884	45.53%
$29,590	$6,724	43.28%
$19,512	$3,796	29.06%
$14,000	$2,252	28.01%
$10,000	$931	33.01%
$7,040	$102	28.01%
$6,456	$0	17.51%
$0	$0	0.00%

Yukon

Bracket	$Tax	+% of excess
$62,193	$19,138	46.55%
$60,469	$18,360	45.10%
$59,180	$17,788	44.37%
$29,590	$6,017	39.78%
$6,456	$0	26.01%
$0	$0	0.00%

To use these tables, in the appropriate jurisdiction find the smallest bracket that is greater than or equal to your taxable income. The amount beside it (under "$Tax") is the tax you would pay if your taxable income were exactly equal to the bracket. If it is higher, multiply the excess by the marginal rate in the next column (under "% of excess").

For example, if your taxable income is $50,000 and you reside in Alberta, your bracket is $44,500 and your tax would be $11,643 + 40.06% of ($50,000 - $44,050), which is $14,027. That is the same amount given in the table on page 245 for a $50,000 taxable income in Alberta, except that figures there are rounded, in this case to $14,000).

The tax you actually pay will be affected by deductions and other factors.

Appendix 3
Investment income: special rates

This appendix will help you:
- compare tax on investment income across Canada
- see what before-tax investment returns give you the same after-tax return

How Investments Are Taxed

Some investment income is taxed differently from other income. The bar chart in this appendix shows **top marginal rates** for the three types of investment income.

Interest and foreign dividends are taxed the same way as most other income. For more details about the rates that apply to interest and foreign dividends, refer to Appendix 1.

Canadian dividends are subject to a gross-up and a tax credit, which together reduce tax (see page 96).

Capital gains also get favourable tax treatment: only three-quarters of a capital gain is included in taxable income and taxed. That portion is taxed at the same rate as interest, so for most purposes the effect is tax at three-quarters the rate that applies to interest. The lifetime capital gains exemption, which was discontinued as of February 22, 1994 (see page 105), may still eliminate tax on $100,000 of capital gains, in some situations. Capital

gains arising on dispositions of qualifying small business corporation (QSBC) shares and certain farming properties may be entitled to an exemption of $500,000 (see page 112).

The results in this Appendix apply to **capital gains in excess of the lifetime exemption**. Capital gains that are partially or completely exempt are treated even more favourably.

Comparing Tax Rates

The bar chart shows the variation in top marginal rates for different types of investment. In all jurisdictions, the top marginal rate for capital gains is, in effect, three-quarters of the rate for interest income. For most jurisdictions, the top marginal rate for Canadian dividends works out to approximately 67.5% of the rate for interest income. However, as the bar chart reveals, the

1995 Top marginal rates [%] →

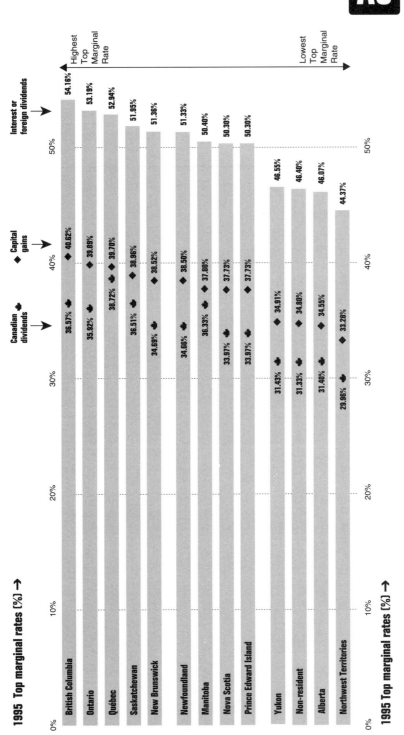

Appendix 3
Investment income: special rates

Before-tax returns required to match 6% or $100 interest

1995	Taxable income = $50,000				Taxable income = $100,000			
	Canadian dividends		Capital gains		Canadian dividends		Capital gains	
British Columbia	4.74%	$79.03	5.13%	$85.49	4.34%	$72.27	4.63%	$77.20
Ontario	4.68%	$78.03	5.08%	$84.75	4.38%	$73.05	4.67%	$77.88
Québec	4.71%	$78.44	4.87%	$81.13	4.61%	$76.81	4.68%	$78.05
Saskatchewan	4.62%	$77.08	4.96%	$82.72	4.54%	$75.69	4.72%	$78.73
New Brunswick	4.62%	$76.92	5.03%	$83.90	4.47%	$74.46	4.75%	$79.11
Newfoundland	4.56%	$75.97	4.99%	$83.18	4.47%	$74.49	4.75%	$79.13
Manitoba	4.74%	$79.05	5.00%	$83.41	4.67%	$77.91	4.78%	$79.74
Nova Scotia	4.67%	$77.76	5.07%	$84.54	4.52%	$75.26	4.79%	$79.81
Prince Edward Island	4.67%	$77.76	5.07%	$84.54	4.52%	$75.26	4.79%	$79.81
Yukon	4.77%	$79.47	5.15%	$85.83	4.68%	$77.96	4.93%	$82.12
Non-resident	4.75%	$79.12	5.13%	$85.56	4.68%	$78.06	4.93%	$82.21
Alberta	4.78%	$79.62	5.14%	$85.69	4.72%	$78.61	4.94%	$82.40
Northwest Territories	4.88%	$81.33	5.21%	$86.84	4.77%	$79.43	5.00%	$83.38

Highest Top Marginal Rate

Lowest Top Marginal Rate

advantage of Canadian dividends over capital gains is noticeably smaller in Québec and Manitoba. Québec's dividend tax credit is less generous than the provincial portion in other provinces. Manitoba has a large flat tax that has a side-effect of reducing the differential between Canadian dividends and capital gains. Saskatchewan's flat tax has a smaller effect, and Alberta's still smaller flat tax reduces the advantage of Canadian dividends only slightly.

Comparing After-Tax Investment Returns

The table on page 249 shows how the different tax treatments of investments can affect investment decisions. For different types of investment, the table answers a realistic question: **What before-tax return must I get to end up with the same after-tax result?** As a benchmark investment, the chart assumes a 6% before-tax return in the form of interest. A $100 interest amount is included as an alternative benchmark.

For example, suppose your taxable income is in the top bracket (say $100,000) and you earn **$100 interest** on a $1,666.67 investment (a 6% before-tax return). In Ontario you would pay tax at a 53.19% marginal rate. You keep $46.81, an after-tax return of about 2.81%. To earn the identical after-tax return from the same $1,666.67 capital, you would need a **Canadian dividend of only $73.05** (which works out to 4.38%). If, instead, you had a capital gain of $77.88 on an asset you had bought for $1,666.67 a year earlier, (a 4.67% before-tax gain), you would also have a 2.81% return after tax. You would again retain the $46.81 after tax – the same as from the $100 of interest or the $73.71 Canadian dividend.

These results vary somewhat by province, as the table shows, as well as by the taxpayer's tax bracket.

Appendix 4
Federal marginal rates: tax and surtax

This appendix will help you:
- find the federal 1995 marginal tax rate that applies to you
- see how the federal surtax affects you

Federal marginal rates are a key element in the personal income tax rate structure in Canada. Not only the federal portion of your taxes depends on federal marginal rates. Provincial and territorial income taxes are also based on federal rates (see Appendix 5). Québec is the only exception.

Components of Federal Rates

Your federal marginal tax rate is the percentage of the last (or next) dollar you earn that is paid as federal income tax. To find out your federal marginal rate, read the entry in the chart that corresponds to your **taxable income**.

The top portion of the chart shows the three basic federal marginal rates of 17% (on taxable income up to $29,590), 26% (on taxable income between $29,590 and $59,180) and 29% (on taxable income above $59,180).

However, as the chart shows, these three rates turn into a set of five rates.

The **basic personal credit** ($1,098) eliminates tax on the first $6,456 of taxable income for all taxpayers, creating the 0% marginal rate (because $1,098 is 17% of $6,456). This credit is indexed, increasing annually when inflation exceeds a threshold. Low inflation has kept the basic credit the same for 1995 as it was for 1994, 1993 and 1992. Any other non-refundable credits to which you may be entitled increase the amount of income on which the marginal tax rate is zero.

The general **federal surtax** rate is 3% of basic federal tax. That adds, for example, 0.51% to the 17% bottom marginal rate (17% x 3% = 0.51%). When your basic federal tax reaches $12,500, an additional "high-earner" surtax of 5% of basic federal tax in excess of $12,500 applies. This occurs at a taxable income of $62,195, assuming you have only the basic personal credit. So, at a taxable income above $62,195, the total federal surtax

1995 Federal marginal rates (including the federal surtax)

Taxable income →

Except Québec

	$0	$6,456	$29,590	$59,180	$62,195
Before basic personal credit and federal surtax					
After basic personal credit	0%	17%	26%	29%	
Federal surtax rates		x 3%		x 8% (3% + 5% "high-earner" surtax)	
Federal surtax (addition to marginal rates)		0.51%	0.78%	0.87%	2.32%
Total (except Québec)	0%	17.51%	26.78%	29.87%	31.32%

Québec

Federal rates after Québec abatement	14.195% (17% x 0.835)	21.71% (26% x 0.835)	24.215% (29% x 0.835)	
Federal surtax (addition to marginal rates)	0%	0.51%	0.78%	0.87%	2.32%
Total (Québec)	14.705%	22.49%	25.085%	26.535%

Taxable income →

$0 $10,000 $20,000 $30,000 $40,000 $50,000 $60,000 $70,000 $80,000 $90,000 $100,000

Appendix 4
Federal marginal rates: tax and surtax

is 8%. Any other non-refundable credits you may be able to claim will increase the taxable income you can have before the higher "high-earner" federal surtax affects you. On account of the two levels of federal surtax, the 29% marginal rate turns into two rates: 29.87% and 31.32%.

Québec

For Québec residents, the **Québec abatement** reduces basic federal tax by 16.5%. This, in effect, reduces federal marginal rates to 83.5% of their original levels. For example, the top federal rate of 29% becomes 24.215%. The federal surtax, however, is the same for Québec residents as it is for residents of other jurisdictions.

Other Factors Affecting Tax Rates

The federal marginal rates shown in this Appendix are central to the calculation of your tax bill. However, **the income tax you pay cannot be determined directly from federal marginal rates.** Your taxes will be substantially affected by:

- provincial taxes and surtaxes (discussed in Appendices 4 and 5), which add roughly half as much again to your tax bill.

- non-refundable tax credits to which you may be entitled (see page 182), which may reduce or even eliminate your income tax liability; and

- the types of income you have, since capital gains and some dividend income are taxed differently (see Appendix 3).

Appendix 5
Provincial marginal rates: tax and surtax

Provincial marginal rates (before surtaxes) are simply a proportion of pre-surtax federal marginal rates, except for Québec.

Québec sets its own rates and brackets. The Personal Tax Flowchart (page 183) explains how Québec's approach differs.

Provincial Tax Rates

For jurisdictions other than Québec, the proportion (or factor) is shown down the left of the chart on the facing page. The factors range from 45% in the Northwest Territories to 69% in Newfoundland. (Rates for the territories and non-residents are considered "provincial rates" in this book.) The body of the chart shows Québec's rates and the rates elsewhere (the factor multiplied by the federal marginal rates from Appendix 4).

Provincial Surtaxes

Jurisdictions other than Newfoundland and the Northwest Territories impose surtaxes. Non-residents of Canada and residents of Newfoundland or the Northwest Territories face no surtaxes other than the federal ones.

The chart on page 258 shows the effect of provincial surtaxes on marginal rates for all jurisdictions and levels of taxable income. The table on page 259 shows the rates and brackets from which these results are derived.

Surtaxes come in two main varieties: "regular" surtaxes and flat taxes. Regular surtaxes are calculated as a percentage of provincial (or territorial) tax above a stated amount (e.g., 8% of provincial tax in excess of $13,500 in New Brunswick). Except for Québec, this results in provincial surtaxes being a percentage of federal tax (e.g, 8% x 64% x 29% = 1.4848% in New Brunswick). As a consequence, the amount that a "regular" provincial surtax adds to marginal rates increases whenever taxable income reaches a higher federal bracket. Flat taxes

1995 Provincial marginal rates (before surtax)

Taxable income →

Province	Provincial tax as % of basic federal tax	$0	$6,456	$14,000	$23,000	$29,550	$50,000	$59,180
British Columbia*	52.5%		8.93%*			13.65%		15.23%
Ontario*	58%		9.86%*			15.08%		16.82%
Québec*	n/a	0%	19%*	21%*			23%*	24%
Saskatchewan*	50%		8.5%*			13%		14.5%
New Brunswick	64%		10.88%			16.64%		18.56%
Newfoundland	69%		11.73%			17.94%		20.01%
Manitoba*	52%	0%	8.84%*			13.52%		15.08%
Nova Scotia*	59.5%		10.12%			15.47%		17.26%
Prince Edward Island	59.5%		10.12%			15.47%		17.26%
Yukon	50%	0%	8.5%			13%		14.5%
Non-resident	52%		8.84%			13.52%		15.08%
Alberta*	45.5%		7.74%*			11.83%		13.2%
Northwest Territories**	45%		7.65%**			11.7%**		13.05%**

Axis markers: $0 $10,000 $20,000 $30,000 $40,000 $50,000 $60,000 $70,000 $80,000 $90,000 $100,000

* Provincial tax reductions will alter the marginal rates for low-income taxpayers in Alberta, British Columbia, Manitoba, Nova Scotia, Ontario and Saskatchewan. Québec taxpayers with incomes up to about $53,000 are affected.

** These results do not reflect the Northwest Territories' Cost of Living Tax Credit, which reduces tax payable and creates additional brackets.

1995 Provincial surtaxes and flat taxes – effect on marginal rates

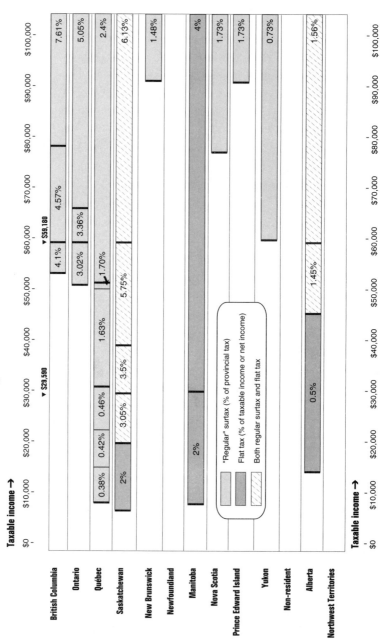

Taxable income →

$0	$10,000	$20,000	$30,000	$40,000	$50,000	$60,000	$70,000	$80,000	$90,000	$100,000

British Columbia ▼$29,590 ▼$59,180 4.1% 4.57% 7.61%

Ontario 0.38% 0.42% 0.46% 3.02% 3.36% 5.05%

Quebec 1.63% 1.70% 2.4%

Saskatchewan 2% 3.05% 3.5% 5.75% 6.13%

New Brunswick 1.48%

Newfoundland

Manitoba 2% 4%

Nova Scotia 1.73%

Prince Edward Island 1.73%

Yukon 0.73%

Non-resident

Alberta 0.5% 1.45% 1.56%

Northwest Territories

"Regular" surtax (% of provincial tax)

Flat tax (% of taxable income or net income)

Both regular surtax and flat tax

Taxable income →

$0	$10,000	$20,000	$30,000	$40,000	$50,000	$60,000	$70,000	$80,000	$90,000	$100,000

	Rates (% of Provincial tax)	"Regular" surtax			Flat tax	
		Thresholds Provincial Tax	Taxable income	Resulting addition to marginal rate	Rates	Thresholds (taxable or net income)
British Columbia	30.0% 50.0%	$5,300 $9,000	$53,292 $78,203	4.095% to 4.5675% 7.6125%		
Ontario	20.0% 30.0%	$5,500 $8,000	$50,936 $66,652	3.016% to 3.364% 5.046%	n/a	
Québec	2.0% 7.1% 10.0%	$0 $5,000 $10,000	$8,348 $31,000 $52,625	0.38% to 0.46% 1.633% to 1.704% 2.4%		
Saskatchewan	10.0% 25.0%	$1,500 $4,000	$19,512 $39,202	1.05% to 1.5% 3.75% to 4.125%	2.00%	$7,040*
New Brunswick	8.0%	$13,500	$91,827	1.4848%	n/a	
Newfoundland			n/a			
Manitoba			n/a		2.00% 4.00%	$7,794* $30,000
Nova Scotia	10.0%	$10,000	$77,044	1.7255%		
Prince Edward Island	10.0%	$12,500	$91,532	1.7255%	n/a	
Yukon	5.0%	$6,000	$60,469	0.725%		
Non-resident			n/a			
Alberta	8.0%	$3,500	$44,050	0.9464% to 1.0556%	0.50%	$9,545*
Northwest Territories			n/a			

*All flat taxes (i.e., in Saskatchewan, Manitoba and Alberta) would apply to the first dollar of taxable or net income, except that the tax reductions for low income earners have the effect of preventing the flat taxes from applying until taxable income reaches at least the levels shown.

Appendix 5
Provincial marginal rates: tax and surtax

are based on taxable income or net income, and are therefore independent of federal brackets.

In Québec, provincial tax is not a percentage of federal tax, so federal brackets affect neither the amount that the provincial surtax adds to marginal rates nor the thresholds at which particular rates take effect. However, provincial brackets have the equivalent result.

Some provinces have surtaxes with more than one threshold (expressed as an amount of provincial tax), each one creating a new surtax bracket.

Provincial surtaxes are notable for their variety in structure and level. At the top tax bracket, British Columbia's adds 7.61% to marginal rates, while the Yukon's adds only 0.73%. Saskatchewan's affects taxable incomes as low as $7,040, while New Brunswick's affects only taxable incomes over $91,827.

Appendix 1 combines provincial taxes and surtaxes with the federal tax and the federal surtaxes set out in Appendix 4.

Alberta, British Columbia, Manitoba, Nova Scotia, Ontario, Saskatchewan and Québec have **tax reductions**

that, in effect, create additional marginal rates for those with relatively low taxable incomes. The reductions eliminate provincial income tax (but not federal income tax) for taxable incomes immediately above $6,456. However, taxpayers with slightly larger taxable incomes face a higher than normal marginal tax rate that, in effect, undoes the benefit of the provincial tax reduction. The result is that taxpayers can ignore the reductions if their taxable incomes are above a certain level (roughly $53,000 in Québec, and $10,000 to $22,000 for the other provinces that have the reductions).

Provincial surtaxes can affect marginal rates as much as the variation in the provincial factors that are used to calculate provincial tax. For example, at 69% Newfoundland's factor is the highest in the country, while Saskatchewan's is among the lowest, just 50%. That difference gives Newfoundland a top combined marginal rate before provincial surtaxes that is 5.51% higher than Saskatchewan's. But at top rates, Saskatchewan's surtax adds 6.125% to its marginal rates, yielding a top marginal rate more than 0.6% higher than Newfoundland's.

This appendix will help you:
- assess the value of various credits
- compare Québec credits with credits in other jurisdictions

Appendix 6
Credits and amounts that reduce your taxes

Assumptions

The tax saving shown in the table (both for Québec and elsewhere) assumes that the entire credit can be used to reduce taxes. Because these credits are non-refundable, this will not be true if total credits exceed taxes otherwise payable. In that case the value of the credit is limited to the amount of tax.

Jurisdictions Other than Québec

One group of columns in the table shows **approximate results for jurisdictions other than Québec**. (Instead of showing a different result for each province, the table is based on provincial tax calculated as a representative factor of 55% of basic federal tax. Results for each jurisdiction will vary (see Appendix 5).

Federal credits are generally 17% of federal amounts or claims. Federal amounts are indexed annually when inflation exceeds a threshold.

Québec

Credits that apply in Québec are shown in a separate group of columns. For Québec, the federal credit is, in effect, reduced by 16.5% by the Québec abatement (see Appendix 4), so that in most cases the credit drops to 14.2% of the federal amounts or claims, from the 17% (100% – 16.5%) x 17%.

Other differences for Québec residents include:

- the continued use of a deduction (rather than credits) for tuition and education expenses;

- the continued availability of credits for dependants under 18 years of age;

Credits and amounts that reduce your 1995 taxes

	Federal amount or claim	Other than Québec		Québec			Special characteristics
		Federal credit	Saving*	Credit Federal**	Québec	Saving*	
Basic personal	$6,456	$1,098	$1,735	$917	$1,180	$2,130	Available to every taxpayer
Married / Equivalent to married	$5,380	$915	$1,445	$764	n/a	$1,971	
Dependants 18 or over if infirm	$1,583	$269	$425	$225	$1,180	$1,413	May be reduced if income of spouse or dependant exceeds
Dependants under 18 first / each additional	No federal credit available.				$520	$480	
Single parent	See page 196 re the child tax benefit.				$260	$210	Québec only
Living alone							
Disability/mental or physical impairment	$4,233	$720	$1,137	$601	$440	$1,063	Unused portion is transferable in some circumstances to spouse, parent, grandparent, or to child supporting a disabled parent or grandparent.
Age 65 and over	$3,482	$592	$935	$494		$952	For federal purposes, age credit is reduced above certain income levels. Outside Québec, maximum $680 is transferable for tuition and education combined (see page 185).
Education	up to $80 per month	up to $14 per month	up to $22 per month	up to $11 per month	$330 per semester up to $660	up to $809	
Tuition fees	minimum $100 per institution				deduction	depends on marginal rate	Tuition deduction can be claimed only by the student for Québec purposes.
Pension income	up to $1,000	up to $170	up to $269	up to $142	up to $200	up to $347	
Medical expenses	over lesser of $1,614 and 3% of net income	17% ... 25.9%		14.2% 20% 34.7%			Not transferable, but one spouse may claim the other's medical expenses or charitable donations (see page 186). Effective 1993, Québec's deductions for charitable donations, CPP/QPP and UI were converted into credits.
CPP/QPP and UI premiums	limited to maximum premium for the year	up to $349	up to $551	up to $292	up to $410	up to $592	
Charitable donations first $200 / over $200	up to 20% of net income	29% 45.8%		24.2% 45%		45%	

* The combined saving is an approximate reduction in taxes. It is calculated incorporating the federal surtax at the lower rate (3% of basic federal tax). For jurisdictions other than Québec, savings in provincial tax are approximated as 55% of the federal credit (see Appendix 5). For Québec, the saving related to the federal surtax is added to the federal credit and the Québec credit to yield the combined saving.

Taxpayers whose taxable incomes exceed $62,195 pay the federal surtax at a rate of 8% of basic federal tax. Their benefit from a credit will be higher by 5% of the full federal credit (not reduced by the Québec abatement) shown in the table.

** The Québec abatement reduces the federal credit by 16.5%.

- no transferability of tuition fee deduction;

- supporting person may claim credit for student's post-secondary studies;

- the existence of credits for persons living alone and single parents; and

- the absence of the "equivalent-to-married" credit (apart from the federal portion).

Glossary of tax abbreviations

ABIL	Allowable business investment loss
AMT	Alternative minimum tax
AVC	Additional voluntary contributions
BIL	Business investment loss
CCA	Capital cost allowance
CCPC	Canadian-controlled private corporation
CIP	Cooperative investment plan (Québec)
CNIL	Cumulative net investment loss
CPP	Canada Pension Plan
DPSP	Deferred profit sharing plan
FST	Federal sales tax
GST	Goods and Services Tax
IRA	Individual retirement account (U.S.)
MURB	Multiple-unit residential building
OAS	Old age security
PA	Pension adjustment
PSPA	Past service pension adjustment
PST	Provincial sales tax
QBIC	Québec business investment company
QPP	Québec Pension Plan
QSBC	Qualifying small business corporation
QSSP	Québec stock savings plan
RPP	Registered pension plan
RRIF	Registered retirement income fund
RRSP	Registered retirement savings plan
SBC	Small business corporation
SDI	Société de développement industriel du Québec
SIN	Social Insurance Number
UCC	Undepreciated capital cost
UI	Unemployment insurance

Price Waterhouse offices across Canada

Halifax, N.S. B3J 3N4
1801 Hollis Street
Suite 900
Telephone: (902) 420 1900
Telecopier: (902) 420 1755

Québec (Québec) G1V 4W2
Tour de la Cité (Sainte-Foy)
870 - 2600, boul. Laurier
Telephone: (418) 658 5782
Telecopier: (418) 656 6640

Montréal (Québec) H3B 2G4
1250, boul. René-Lévesque ouest
Bureau 3500
Telephone: (514) 938 5600
Telecopier: (514) 938 5709

Ottawa, Ontario K2P 2K3
Barrister House
180 Elgin Street
Suite 1100
Telephone: (613) 238 8200
Telecopier: (613) 238 4798

Toronto, Ontario M5X 1H7
1 First Canadian Place
Suite 3300
Box 190
Telephone: (416) 863 1133
Telecopier: (416) 365 8151

Metro Toronto North M2M 4K7
5700 Yonge Street
Suite 1900
Telephone: (416) 218 1500
Telecopier: (416) 218 1499

Mississauga, Ontario L4Z 3M3
Mississauga Executive Centre
Suite 1100
One Robert Speck Parkway
Telephone: (905) 272 1200
Telecopier: (905) 272 3937

Hamilton, Ontario L8N 3R1
4 Hughson Street South
P.O. Box 1018
Telephone: (905) 525 9650
Telecopier: (905) 525 8200

Kitchener, Ontario N2G 4W1
Canada Trust Centre, Suite 900
55 King Street West
Telephone: (519) 579 6300
Telecopier: (519) 579 8701

London, Ontario N6B 3L1
Canada Trust Tower
275 Dundas Street, Suite 1500
Telephone: (519) 679 9160
Telecopier: (519) 679 1435

Windsor, Ontario N9A 6T3
Bank of Commerce Building
100 Ouellette Avenue
Suite 1200
Telephone: (519) 258 6052
Telecopier: (519) 258 5457

Winnipeg, Manitoba R3B 0X7
2200 One Lombard Place
Telephone: (204) 943 7321
Telecopier: (204) 943 7774

Regina, Saskatchewan S4P 2C2
Bank of Commerce Building
1867 Hamilton Street, Suite 1250
Telephone: (306) 757 5917
Telecopier: (306) 757 7956

Saskatoon, Saskatchewan S7K 7E6
The Princeton Tower
123 - 2nd Avenue South
Suite 400
Telephone: (306) 244 6164
Telecopier: (306) 653 3813

Calgary, Alberta T2P 3V7
425 - 1st Street S.W.
Suite 1200
Telephone: (403) 267 1200
Telecopier: (403) 264 4745

Calgary, Alberta T2W 4X9
(Calgary South Office)
10201 Southport Road S.W.
Suite 1000, Southland Plaza
Telephone: (403) 974 5300
Telecopier: (403) 258 1121

Edmonton, Alberta T5J 2Z1
1501 Toronto Dominion Tower
Edmonton Centre
Telephone: (403) 493 8200
Telecopier: (403) 428 8069

Kamloops, B.C. V2C 6P5
200 - 206 Seymour Street
Telephone: (604) 372 5551
Telecopier: (604) 372 1422

Vancouver, B.C. V6B 5A5
Price Waterhouse Centre
601 West Hastings Street
Suite 1400
Telephone: (604) 682 4711
Telecopier: (604) 443 2635

Surrey, B.C. V3T 5T3
Station Tower, Gateway
13401 - 108th Avenue
Suite 1600
Telephone: (604) 582 3400
Telecopier: (604) 582 3401

Richmond, B.C. V6X 3J6
5611 Cooney Road
Suite 100
Telephone: (604) 231 5500
Telecopier: (604) 231 5599

Index

Index

Index

Index